Chatty Cathy™ and Her Talking Friends

An Unauthorized Guide for Collectors

Sean Kettelkamp

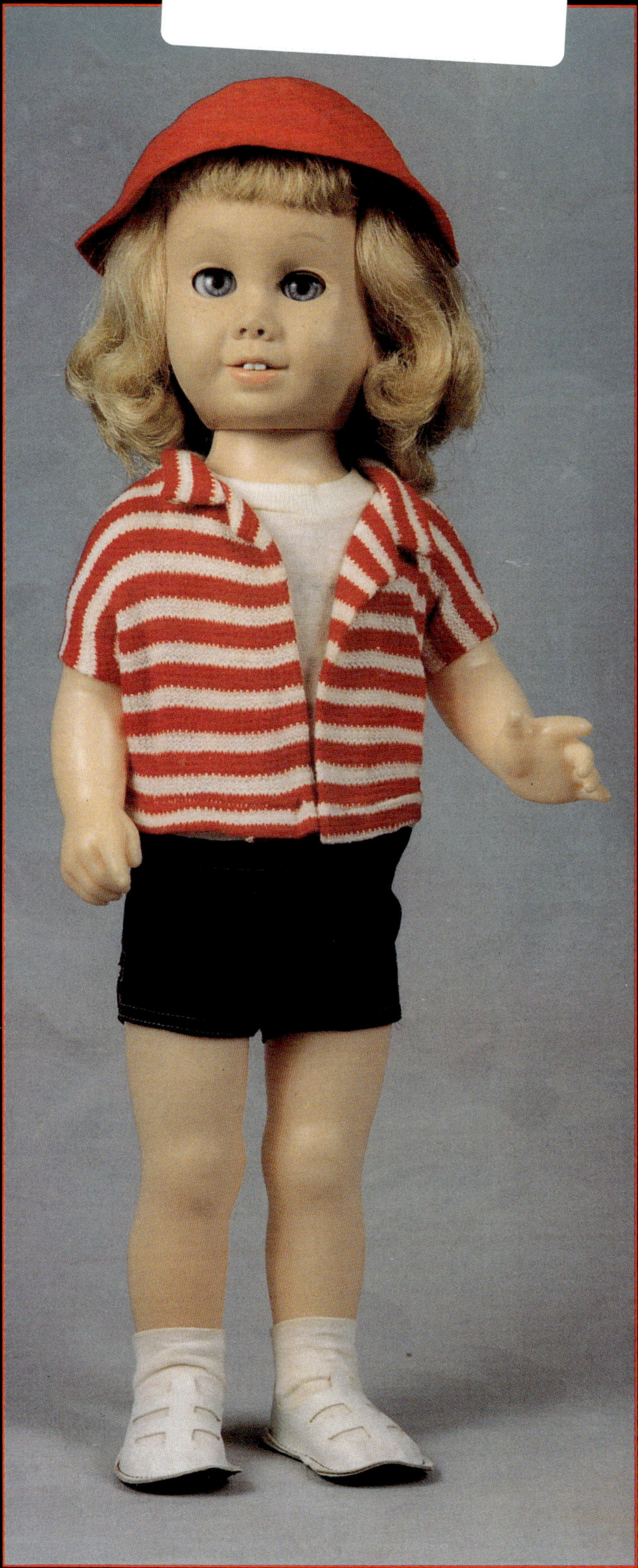

4880 Lower Valley Road, Atglen, PA 19310 USA

Mattel, Inc. did not authorize this book nor furnish or approve any of the information contained therein. This book is derived from the author's independent research.

"Baby Small Talk," Registered Trademark of Mattel, Inc.
"Baby Small Walk," Registered Trademark of Mattel, Inc.
"Baby Tender Love," Registered Trademark of Mattel, Inc.
"Baby's Hungry," Registered Trademark of Mattel, Inc. (Applicant)
"Barbie," Registered Trademark of Mattel, Inc.
"Becky," Registered Trademark of Mattel, Inc.
"Chatter Chums," Registered Trademark of Mattel, Inc.
"Chatty Cathy," Registered Trademark of Mattel, Inc. (Applicant)
"Cynthia," Registered Trademark of Mattel, Inc.
"Dancerina," Registered Trademark of Mattel, Inc.
"Dee Dee," Registered Trademark of Mattel, Inc.
"Drowsy," Registered Trademark of Mattel, Inc.
"Leroy Lion," Registered Trademark of Mattel, Inc.
"Lilac & Lovely," Registered Trademark of Mattel, Inc.
"Matty," Registered Trademark of Mattel, Inc.
"Patty Peach," Registered Trademark of Mattel, Inc.
"Quick Curl," Registered Trademark of Mattel, Inc.
"See 'n Say," Registered Trademark of Mattel, Inc.
"Sister Small-Talk," Registered Trademark of Mattel, Inc.
"Super Barbie," Trademark Pending; Mattel, Inc. (Applicant)
"T-Bone," Trademark Pending; Mattel, Inc. (Applicant)
"Talking Friends Mother Goose," Trademark Pending; Mattel, Inc. (Applicant)

"The Adventures of Rocky and Bullwinkle and Friends," Registered Trademark of Ward Productions, Inc.
"Baby Beans," Registered Trademark of Adolph Eddy Goldfarb.
"Baby First Steps," Registered Trademark of Irwin Toy Limited.
"Baby Secrets," Registered Trademark of Cal R & D, Inc.

"Baby Whispers," Registered Trademark of Whispers, Inc.
"Beany & Cecil," Registered Trademark of Bob Clampett Productions Inc. (Applicant)
"Bouncy Baby," Trademark Pending; Meyer/Glass Design Ltd. (Applicant)
"Bozo," Registered Trademark of Larry Harmon Pictures Corporation.
"Bugs Bunny," Registered Trademark of Time Warner Entertainment Company, L.P.
"Captain Kangaroo," Registered Trademark of Robert Keeshan Associates, Inc.
"Casper," Registered Trademark of Harvey Comics, Inc.
"Cat in the Hat," Registered Trademark of Dr. Seuss Enterprises, L.P. (Applicant)
"Cheerful Tearful," Registered Trademark of Catalina Toys, Inc.
"Donald Duck," Registered Trademark of The Walt Disney Company.
"Dottie," Registered Trademark of Jelly Bean Jungle Productions, Inc.
"Googlies," Registered Trademark of Hasbro, Inc.
"Horton the Elephant," Registered Trademark of Dr. Seuss Enterprises, L.P.
"Humpty Dumpty," Registered Trademark of Kessler Marketing Group, Inc.
"King Kong," Registered Trademark of Mego Corp.
"Mickey Mouse," Registered Trademark of The Walt Disney Company.
"Mister Ed," Registered Trademark of Scooter Productions, Inc. (Applicant)
"Mister Ed," Registered Trademark of Bobby R. Butler, Jr. and Janet C. Butler.
"The Munsters," Registered Trademark of Universal City Studios, Inc.
"My Gram-ma," Registered Trademark of Berkoh Company, Inc.
"The Pink Panther," Registered Trademark of United Artists Corporation
"Popeye," Registered Trademark of The Hearst Corporation.
"Porky Pig," Registered Trademark of Time Warner Entertainment Company.
"Saucy Walker," Registered Trademark of Ideal Toy Corp.
"Scooby Doo," Registered Trademark of Hanna-Barbera Productions, Inc.
"Splish Splash Baby Play-a-lot," Trademark Pending; Unimax Toys Limited (Applicant)
"The Talking Mother Goose," Registered Trademark of Playskool, Inc.
"Tatterhood," Registered Trademark of Jillayne Waite.
"Tinkerbell," Registered Trademark of Tom Fields, Ltd.
"Tom & Jerry," Registered Trademark of Turner Entertainment Co.
"Woody Woodpecker," Registered Trademark of Walter Lantz Productions, Inc.
"Yertle the Turtle," Registered Trademark of Dr. Seuss Enterprises, L.P. (Applicant)

Copyright © 1998 by Sean Kettelkamp
Library of Congress Catalog Card Number: 97-80233

All rights reserved. No part of this work may be reproduced or used in any form or by any means—graphic, electronic, or mechanical, including photocopying or information storage and retrieval systems—without written permission from the copyright holder.

Book Design by: Laurie A. Smucker

ISBN: 0-88740-954-7
Printed in China 1234

Published by Schiffer Publishing Ltd.
4880 Lower Valley Road
Atglen, PA 19310
Phone: (610) 593-1777; Fax: (610) 593-2002
E-mail: schifferbk@aol.com
Please write for a free catalog.
This book may be purchased from the publisher.
Please include $3.95 for shipping.
Try your bookstore first.

We are interested in hearing from authors
with book ideas on related subjects.

Value Guide Information

The values in this book reflect M.I.B. - Mint-in-Box condition. This means that the doll or toy has its wrist tag, warranty card, and booklet, and that any box inserts are present. It also means that the doll or toy is in factory mint condition. Anything less may significantly reduce the value.

A range of dollar values is given for most items. The high end prices are for dolls that are N.R.F.B., or Never Removed From Box, as well as for dolls with hair color other than blonde or eye color other than blue.

For some items, too few exist to formulate an actual value. These items are marked "rare" in the captions.

Contents

Acknowledgments 4

Introduction 5

Chapter 1 - 1960 6

Chapter 2 - 1961 9

Chapter 3 - 1962 16

Chapter 4 - 1963 29

Chapter 5 - 1964 64

Chapter 6 - 1965 66

Chapter 7 - 1966 77

Chapter 8 - 1967 84

Chapter 9 - 1968 91

Chapter 10 - 1969 99

Chapter 11 - 1970 105

Chapter 12 - 1971 114

Chapter 13 - 1972 122

Chapter 14 - 1973 and Beyond 125

Dedication

This book is dedicated to my grandmother, Lola Bateman Kettelkamp, who has been an inspiration my whole life, and to the memory of my mother, Mary Kettelkamp Houdek.

Acknowledgments

Many thanks to all my friends, without whose support none of this would be possible!

Michelle Owens
Cris Johnson
Ben LaBaw
Chuck Klug
Michael Reimer
Sharon Harrington
Rochelle Tucker
Michael Ivanitsky

Graylen Becker
Cyndie Steffen
Michael Izzo
Carmen Tickle
Betsy Houdek Johnson
Brian Houdek
Steven Houdek

And a very special message of gratitude to Ethel Stucky.

Grateful acknowledgment is also due to the following photographers for their contribution to this project and for permission to reprint their photographs. All photographs not otherwise annotated are by Ben LaBaw:

Sean Kettelkamp
Cris Johnson
Chuck Klug
Michael Izzo
Sharon Harrington
Ben LaBaw

All dolls and other items pictured, unless annotated, are from the author's collection.

There is no instant gratification in a work of art.

—I.M. Pei,
Architect

Introduction

In the 1960s Chatty Cathy made a tremendous impact on the toy industry. She was the pioneer that started more than thirty years of pull string talking dolls and toys. She was on the market for six years, making her the second most popular doll of the 1960s after the Barbie doll. Indeed, both Chatty Cathy and Barbie were put out by Mattel Inc. Toy makers, manufactured and marketed in the same manner. Their clothes were made of the same fabrics, designed by the same designers, and sewn by the same seamstresses.

A whole group of Chatty dolls was marketed in the 1960s: Chatty Cathy, Chatty Baby, Charmin' Chatty, Tiny Chatty Baby, Tiny Chatty Brother, and Singin' Chatty. Several plush talking dolls, toys, and puppets were also on the market at that time.

I have been collecting these dolls exclusively for many, many years. Through the years I have gleaned information from a variety of sources, including store catalogues, the original television commercials, and data from the Mattel archives. Several talking dolls and toys from the 1960s are rare, some more than others. Some dolls may be mentioned in the text for which no pictures or illustrations are available. Many non-talking dolls are listed and featured as well. This is to give you, the collector, some perspective of the era and to help you place or identify a doll or toy in your own collection. I hope you will find pleasure in the book. The experience has been a labor of love for me.

Sean Kettelkamp

Chapter 1 - 1960

In 1958, a young engineer named Jack Ryan, working for Mattel Inc. Toy makers, was busy working on and perfecting a small talking mechanism that operated on the same principal as a primitive phonograph. This mechanism was being designed for an as yet unnamed doll.

Mattel, at this time, had its team of artists and designers working on the development of a doll that would personify an American four-year-old girl. When the doll was finally manufactured in 1959, the result was a doll that could talk and say eleven different complete phrases all at random by pulling her "magic ring."

The doll was ultimately named Chatty Cathy, and she made her debut at the American Toy Fair in New York City in February 1960. Mattel had introduced its Barbie doll the year before and followed similar marketing campaigns for both dolls. Over the next five years, several of their outfits were made from the same fabrics, designed by the same designers, and sewn by the same seamstresses. Barbie got off to a slow start and was in for the long haul, but Chatty Cathy was an immediate success.

Chatty Cathy, through her wardrobe and hairstyle, gives us an intimate look at girlhood in the 1960s. The doll itself stands 20" tall and has a molded, durable plastic body with movable arms, legs, and head made of vinyl. She has a protruding tummy and overall chubby figure.

Mattel used a heavy pliable soft vinyl for Chatty Cathy's head. Her rooted saran hair is a combination of different shades of blonde, giving it a more natural look and color, and is cut in a short bob with bangs. Her "go to sleep" eyes have decal inserts that make them appear more lifelike. All Chatty Cathy dolls in the first year had blonde hair and blue eyes.

At a glance, Chatty Cathy's most engaging feature is her face. She has freckles on her cheeks and across her nose, and two inset, slightly buck teeth that hint she may have sucked her thumb. Her right hand is pointing and her left hand is more relaxed. She was available initially in either a red pinafore or a two-tone blue party dress. There were no extra outfits available during the first year. Her overall look is one of genuine warmth and sweetness...completely delightful and adorable!

The talking mechanism that made Chatty Cathy talk is contained in a 3" by 5" black plastic box; inside that box is a 2.5" record. On top of the record is a spool that has a metal coil and the "magic string" wrapped around it. When the "magic string" at the base of Chatty Cathy's neck is pulled, the "magic string" (about nine inches) winds and tightens the metal coil, much like winding a clock. When the ring is released, the record spins, a tiny phonograph needle sitting on the record plays, and Chatty Cathy talks...like magic!!

The black box which houses all this hardware provided a safeguard against omnipresent toy pirates and is sealed inside the torso of the doll. In the center of her chest is a speaker. On all first edition dolls this speaker is covered with flesh colored cloth; in later editions the cloth was discontinued. Later editions also have a mold mark in the center of the lower back, just above the buttocks. The mold mark has the doll's name and patent number, and some have a tiny Mattel symbol. Since she was still unnamed at the time of her manufacture and her patent was being "applied for," the backs of first year dolls are void of any markings.

That first year, Chatty Cathy was packaged in a pink box covered with cartoon pictures of her in situations relating to the phrases she said and bold letters declaring her "**The Talking Doll**." The front of this box opens like a closet, and inside the box along with Chatty Cathy was a tiny shoe horn and a comic booklet introducing her to her new owner. On the back of this booklet are some instructions on how to care for her. It tells how Chatty Cathy wants her hair brushed, but not combed. To keep her clean, she must be wiped with a damp cloth, but "Never, never put her in water or let her insides get wet! These are doctor's order to protect Chatty Cathy's voice." All copyrights on her box and comic booklet are stamped 1959.

All Mattel dolls from the 1960s to the present have paper tags attached to one wrist stating that they are genuine Mattel dolls. Chatty Cathy's wrist tag resembles a little flower basket and is also her warranty card, guaranteeing her talking mechanism for ninety days. The doll's voice was provided by the famous character actress June Foray, who also was the voice of Rocky the Flying Squirrel on the Bullwinkle cartoon series.

When her string is pulled, Chatty Cathy says:
"Let's have a party."
"May I have a cookie?"
"Please change my dress."

"Do you love me?"
"I love you."
"What can we do now?"
"Please brush my hair."
"I'm so tired."
"Will you play with me?"
"Let's play school."
"Give me a kiss."

Needless to say, playing with dolls took on a whole new meaning when Chatty Cathy came along. This doll could actually communicate with you, give lots of fun ideas for games, and provide hours and hours of playtime. She really seemed to be magic!!

1960 #0681 Chatty Cathy, 20" tall, is wearing a two-toned blue party dress with a white eyelet overblouse and eyelet trimmed crinoline. The outfit includes white cotton jersey panties and socks, with blue velvet shoes decorated with multicolored little flowers on the toes. She has a blue ribbon with attached multicolored flowers in her hair. Her original box, wrist tag, and booklet are also shown. $250-300.

A glimpse inside Chatty Cathy's box shows her elusive shoehorn. It was flesh colored, had no markings on it, and was about 1" long. The shoehorn was available in 1960 only. Shoehorn, $50.

1960 #0682 Chatty Cathy, 20" tall, is wearing a red cotton pinafore with attached sheer white voile. This pinafore is worn over a red cotton jumper that has ruffles around the legs. She also has white cotton jersey socks with red velvet shoes decorated with a little red velvet bow and tiny ring of pearls on the toes. In her hair there is a red velvet headband that snaps at the nape of her neck. She is standing with her original box, wrist tag, and booklet. $250-300.

This is Chatty Cathy's red and white pinafore. This dress was only issued in 1960 and was not sold separately. Some have varied patterns in the sheer voile. $20-40.

This was the symbol proudly displayed on all cartons and packages used by Mattel Inc. Toy makers in the 1960s.

These first addition 20" tall Chatty Cathys are shown with a number 3 Barbie doll, 11.5" tall, from 1960. All were issued by Mattel Inc. Toymakers, and through the years many of their clothes were made of the same fabrics. The scale between them is nicely shown here.

Chapter 2 - 1961

In 1961 the basic doll remained the same and Chatty Cathy was more popular than ever. The speaker in the center of her chest was still covered with flesh colored cloth, but due to different manufacturing methods this cloth sometimes fell off, exposing a mass of small holes. The holes are laid out in a hexagonal shape surrounded by a circle where the cloth was attached.

In the center of Chatty Cathy's lower back, just above her buttocks, there is a mold mark imprinted in less than one square inch that looks like this:

```
CHATTY CATHY™
PATENTS PENDING
©MCMLX
BY MATTEL INC.
HAWTHORNE, CALIF.
```

The really big news for 1961 was that Chatty Cathy now had a complete wardrobe, six pretty outfits available separately:

#697 "Playtime"
#696 "Party Coat"
#695 "Nursery School"
#693 "Peppermint Stick"
#691 "Party Dress"
#694 "Sleepytime"

Her clothes, like Barbie's, were of unmatched quality. They had fine tailored finished seams, buttons, and snaps. Some had beautiful silky linings. Each outfit had a name, and all had tags sewn in them with "Chatty Cathy" printed on the tag. Unlike Barbie, Chatty Cathy's outfits were not for fraternity dances and dates. They were trips to the park, birthday parties, and Sunday visits to grandma's house.

In this second year she was packaged in a new aquamarine "display" box that looked as if it were sprinkled with confetti. This new packaging is referred to by collectors as a "window box" because "windows" are cut out of the front and sides. On the lower front of this box the doll introduces herself in bold letters saying, "Hello! I'm Chatty Cathy the **talking doll**. I can really talk!" Inside the box there is also a new booklet showing black and white photographs of her in each of the new outfits. They were the same folders found packaged with each outfit that was sold separately. Her red pinafore dress was discontinued, and a pink and white candy stripe one took its place. The wrist tag and warranty card resembling a little flower basket remained the same.

Mattel introduced three new talking dolls in 1961. They were Matty the talking boy, Sister Belle, and Casper the talking ghost. Matty became famous as "Matty Mattel," the little boy that jumped atop the giant "**M**" in Mattel television commercials and waved and shouted, "You can tell it's Mattel...it's swell!." His sister Belle joined him as host of a popular cartoon show in the early 1960s called *Matty's Funday Funnies*. The inspiration for this twosome was Jack and Jill from the beloved children's nursery rhyme - Matty even wore a little crown! They introduced several cartoon short stories, and one regular feature was Casper the Ghost. Throughout the show, Mattel toy advertisements for Barbie, Chatty Cathy, and other products were duly shown.

These three dolls were quite nicely done. The talking mechanism in the black box was sealed inside their hard molded plastic head. A rather long neck stem allowed the cloth bodies to be attached by a drawstring at the neck. Matty and Sister Belle had yarn hair and some removable clothing. Casper's body in this first edition is made of crisp white terrycloth. This fabric also covers the speaker holes on the back of his head and looks like a hood.

Chatty Cathy got an additional wardrobe in 1961. Packaged on display cards, these outfits were adorable. Nursery School #695 was a particular favorite. The one shown is unusual because white cotton jersey panties were substituted for the standard red cotton ones. $60-75.

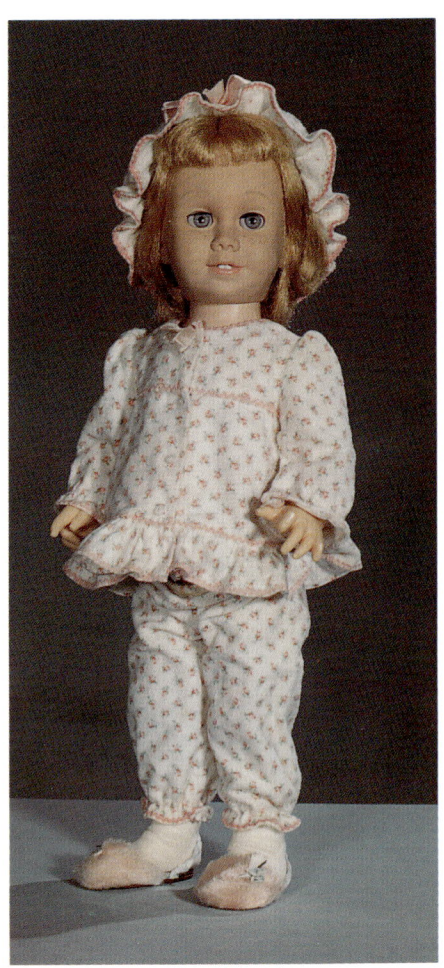

"Sleepytime" #694 was made of white cotton flannel covered with tiny pink rosebuds. The outfit consisted of traditional pajamas with a night cap made of the same material. Pink furry "skuff" slippers completed her nighttime ensemble. $60-75. *Photo by Chuck Klug.*

This beautiful black Chatty Cathy #0742 from 1962 is wearing "Nursery School" #695. Notice the original red panties beneath her dress. *Photo by Chuck Klug.*

This brown-eyed brunette Chatty Cathy is from 1962. She is wearing the popular "Party Coat" #696, a red "velvet" coat with the then fashionable "fur" collar. It is lined with white satin and had a "fur" headband. This coat is made of the same material as the Barbie doll's "Red Flair" #939 and Skipper's "Dress Coat" #1906. $85-100.

Barbie doll's "Red Flair" #939 came out in 1962 and was made of the same red "velvet" as "Party Coat" #696. A matching hat and handbag were included. $120-150.

"Party Coat" #696 had a luxurious "satin" lining; the tag at the neckline says "Chatty Cathy." Remember, all her outfits have tags like this one. $60-75.

The "Red Flair" #939 had a lining that was also the same as "Party Coat" #696.

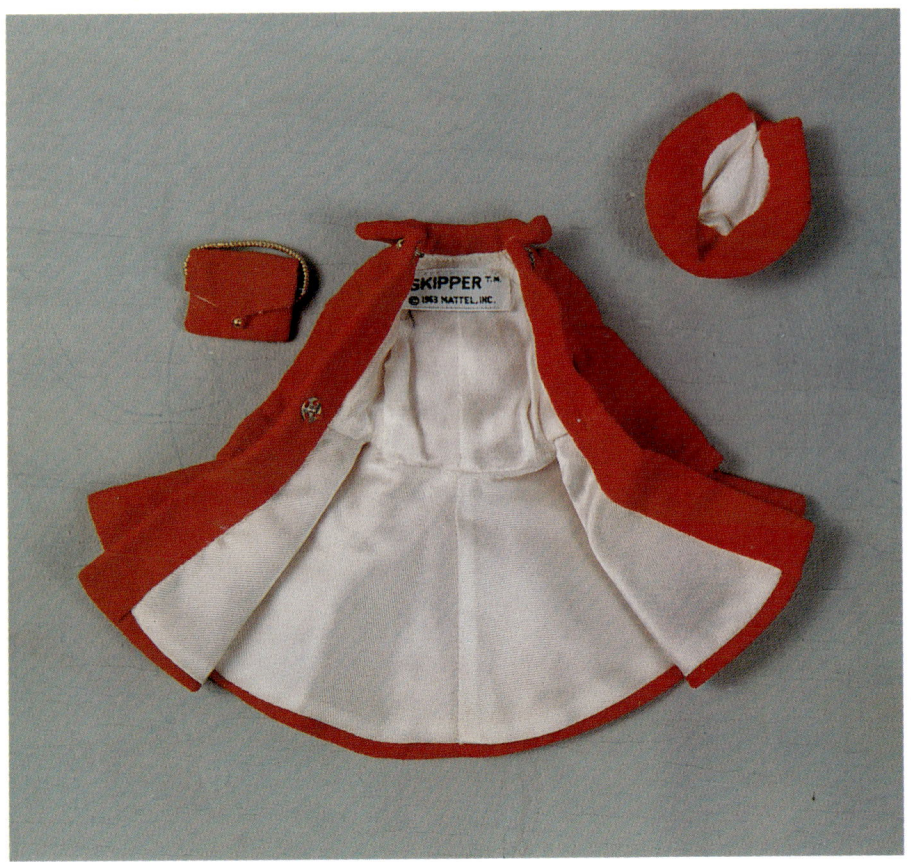

Barbie's little sister Skipper had a coat that was very similar to Chatty Cathy's and was called "Dress Coat" #1906. Skipper and her wardrobe were introduced in 1964 and were very popular. Here you can see that, like Chatty Cathy and Barbie, Skipper got personalized labels in her clothes too! $65-75.

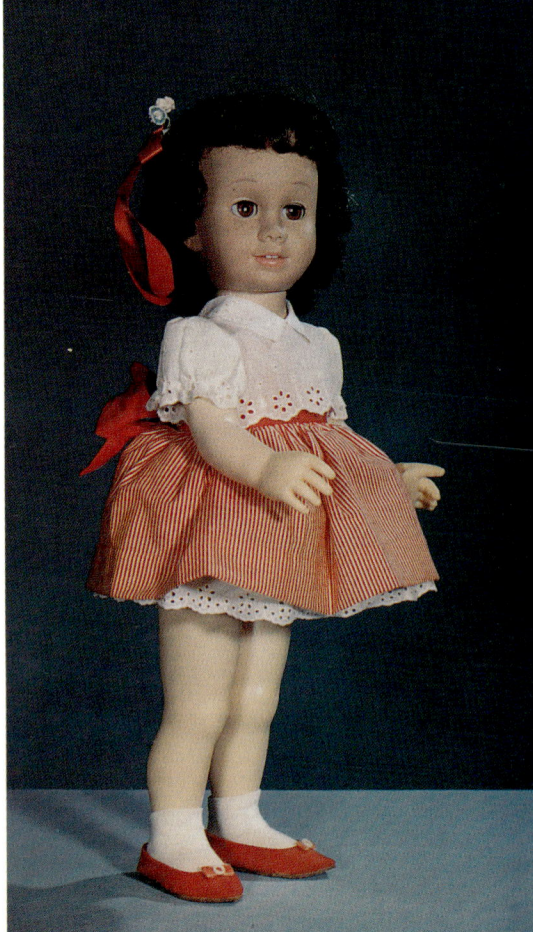

Red "Peppermint Stick" #693 was a great outfit from 1961. It was in the same style as the blue party dress from 1960, but was very rare. The dress had a red bodice with a red and white pinstripe skirt. There was a white eyelet overblouse and an eyelet trimmed crinoline. Red "velvet" shoes and a red ribbon for her hair helped to make this outfit desirable. $125 and up. *Photo by Chuck Klug.*

"Party dress" #691 was another very rare outfit from 1961. This one was a pinafore; the dress was a robin's egg blue Glen Plaid. A white eyelet apron or "pinafore" was worn over the top. She had a blue ribbon for her hair. The blue "velvet" shoes for this outfit were lined with the same Glen Plaid material as her dress. $125 and up. *Photo by Chuck Klug.*

Playtime #697 was a cute outfit for outdoors. It consisted of a pair of blue "denim" shorts and a white t-shirt that snapped in the back. A red and white striped knit jacket, red sunvisor, and white leatherette sandals completed this outfit. Some outfits came packaged with socks, others did not. $60-75.

Sister Belle, #0731, Matty, #0730 and Casper the Ghost #0732 in their original "window boxes".

Matty, #0730, who was also known as Matty Mattel, is shown here with Sister Belle, #0731; both are 17" tall. Their bodies were stuffed and their talking mechanisms were in their heads. Matty's shorts, t-shirt, and crown and Sister Belle's apron are removable. Matty, $400 and up. Sister Belle, $200-250.

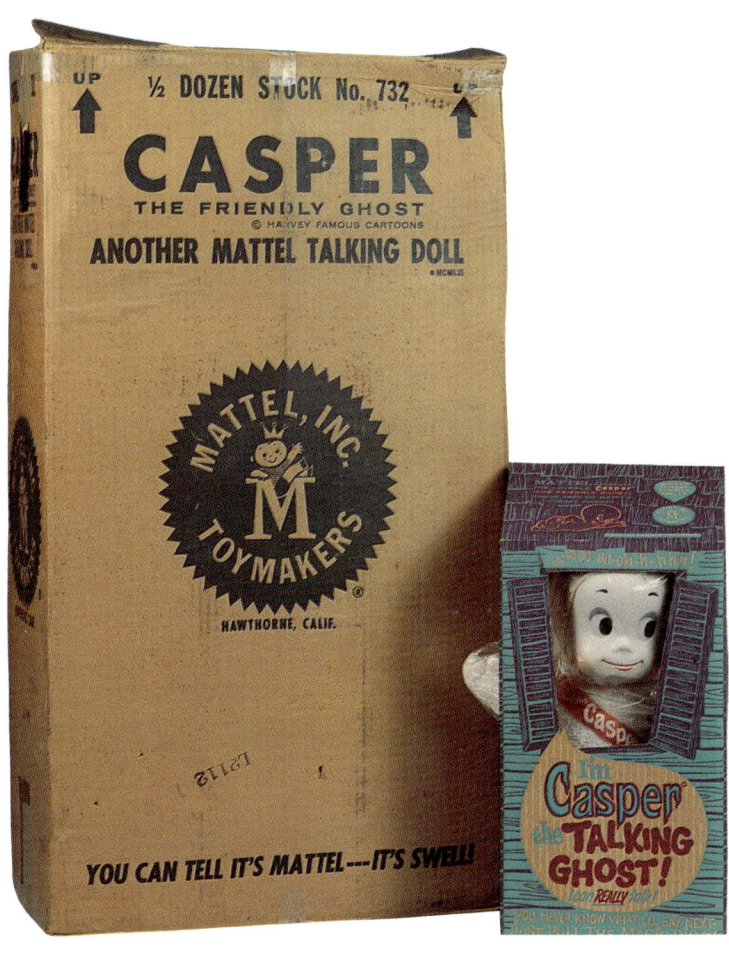

All Mattel dolls were sent to stores in shipping cartons like this one. This one would have contained six Casper the Ghosts! $100 and up for the original shipping carton.

Casper the Ghost, #0732, was made of white terrycloth and stood 15" tall. Like Matty and Sister Belle, his talking mechanism was in his head. Because he had no "hair," a white terrycloth hood covered the speaker holes on the back of his head. $200-250.

Chapter 3 - 1962

As a result of some changes Mattel made to broaden her appeal, Chatty Cathy's popularity continued in 1962. The basic doll remained the same, but now she was available as either a blonde or brunette. The new brunette saran hair, like the blonde, had different shades to make it look more natural. Her decal eyes were now available in brown as well as blue. This lent itself to some wonderful real life combinations. Now little girls could get a Chatty Cathy with brunette hair and brown eyes, brunette hair and blue eyes, and so on. This was an attempt to add diversity to the dolls in general, and for little girls to perhaps own a doll resembling themselves. This made Chatty Cathy a more personal friend.

Modifications in manufacturing and materials were significant too. The heavy pliable soft vinyl used for her head was slowly replaced with a sturdier, more rigid vinyl. Over half the dolls produced in 1962 had the new head. The effect of this new material made Chatty Cathy's head a little smaller and her features more streamlined; if a soft-headed doll stands next to a hard-headed doll, the hard-headed one will be a little shorter.

The talking mechanism sealed inside the doll was now patented. This protection meant that the black plastic box housing the hardware was no longer necessary. The inside of the torso was redesigned to accommodate the record turntable, phonograph needle, and brass eyelets that guide the "magic string." From this year on, the black plastic box (talking mechanism) was used only in plush dolls and toys.

Mattel's preoccupation with covering up the speaker holes in the center of the chest ended this year. The new speaker, or *grille*, as it is now referred to, is a mass of small holes laid out in a hexagonal shape.

One of the more subtle changes in 1962 was to Chatty Cathy's right hand. Some of the dolls produced still had a pointing finger, but a close comparison to the 1960 dolls shows that her other three fingers are not as curved and are instead more relaxed. Some of the fingers on the right hand are all straight. This was done to accommodate the new Chatty Cathy jewelry that was now available separately.

1962 brought some exciting additions to Mattel's talking doll line. Along with the basic Chatty Cathy, a black Chatty Cathy was now available. She was made from the same mold and her black saran hair was cut in the same bob with bangs. She was wearing the pink and white candy stripe dress, now called pink "Peppermint Stick."

The "window" box was used for both the black and white dolls and a new booklet with color photographs of other Mattel toys was included. Her wrist tag was an orange and black circle, resembling a target. This design was also used for most of the other talking doll wrist tags for the next two years. Less than five thousand black Chatty Cathy dolls were manufactured in 1962 and 1963, and are today considered quite rare.

Another wonderful addition was talking Chatty Baby. She was 18" tall and made to resemble an eighteen-month-old baby girl. The durable plastic body used for Chatty Cathy was the same one used for Chatty Baby; she had vinyl arms, legs, and head. The limbs designed for her were chubbier, more infant-like than Chatty Cathy's, and more befitting a toddler. Since the body style has a protruding tummy, her "look" comes together well. She was a hit in the department stores and toy shops in terms of sales, perhaps because these businesses often billed her as Chatty Cathy's baby sister. No such family connection was ever announced officially by Mattel.

Chatty Baby wore a cute two-piece red and white romper set with matching "slipper socks." The packaging was a square box in which she sits, rather than stands, and there is a full color photograph of the doll on the front. A black Chatty Baby was issued, as well as a blonde and a brunette. Their hair was styled in a short pixie cut. There was also an adorable wardrobe consisting of four outfits. Each had a tag sewn in it that said "Chatty Baby." They were available separately:

#0341 "Leotard Set"
#0342 "Sleeper Set"
#0343 "Coverall Set"
#0344 "Playsuit Set"

A dressed doll assortment was now available as well. This meant that both Chatty Cathy and Chatty Baby could be purchased wearing one of their additional outfits. They used the same body mold; as a result, the mold mark changed and remained the same for the rest of their production years:

CHATTY CATHY™
©1960
CHATTY BABY™
©1961
BY MATTEL, INC.
U.S. PAT 3,017,187
OTHER U.S. &
FOREIGN PATENTS PEND.

Cartoon characters Beany Boy, Cecil the Seasick Sea Serpent, and Bugs Bunny (all regulars on *Matty's Funday Funnies*) became talking dolls in 1962. There was even a talking hobby-horse that children could ride called Blaze. The quality, as always with Mattel, was first rate.

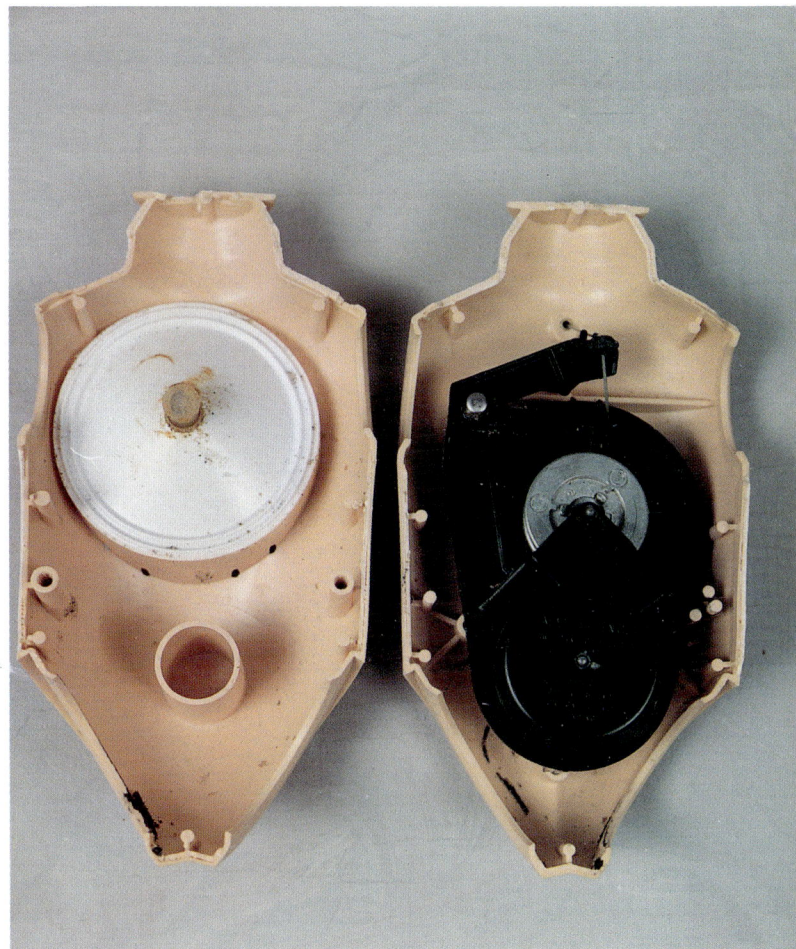

Here is the inside of a Chatty doll. All Mattel talking dolls of the 1960s looked similar to this one inside.

Here's a wonderful 1962 Chatty Cathy with her original box, wrist tag, and folder. She has lovely brunette hair and brown decal eyes. The box was first issued in 1961 and is known to collectors as a "window box." Her dress has pink and white pinstripes and was available separately as pink "Peppermint Stick." The red "Peppermint Stick" had been discontinued after only one year. $350-400.

17

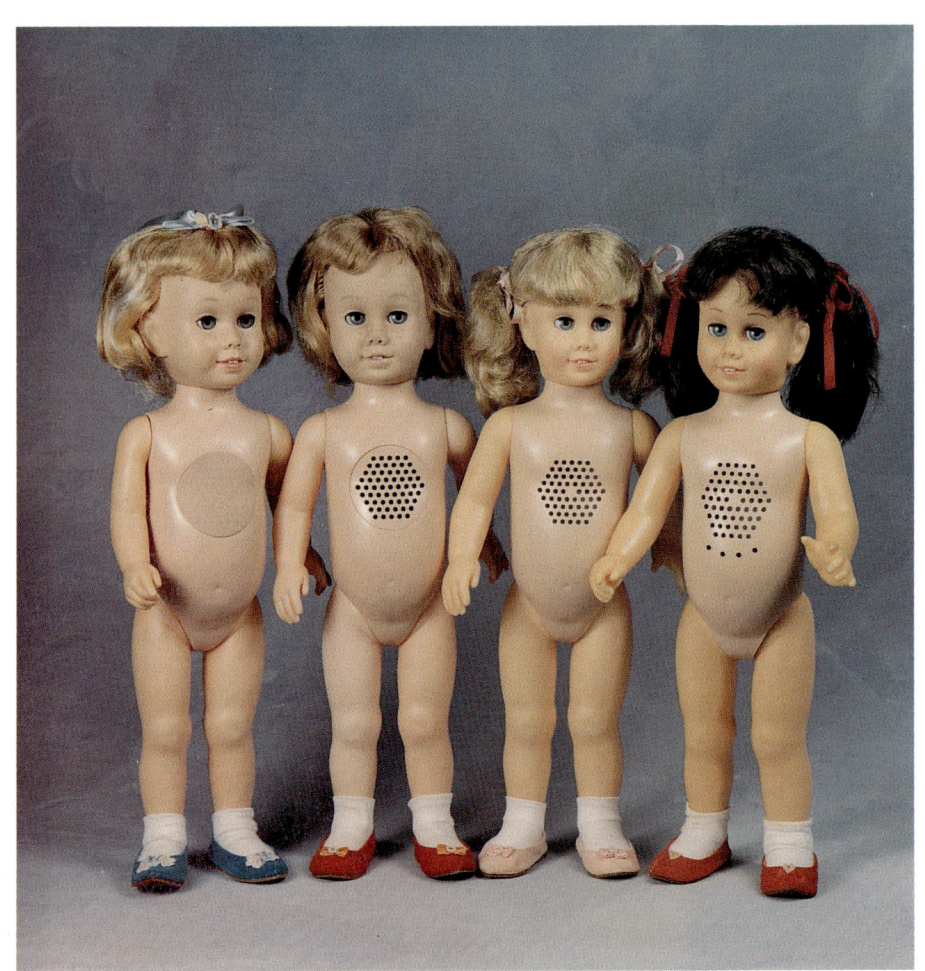

The speaker on the chest of Chatty Cathy went through many transformations. These changes also help determine the date of the doll. The doll on the left is from 1960-61; the speaker is covered with flesh colored cloth. The next doll is from early 1962, we can see the grille, or speaker holes. The grille is surrounded by a circle where the flesh colored cloth used to be attached. From late 1962 to early 1963, as shown on the doll third from left, the speaker holes no longer had the circle surrounding them. And lastly, the doll on the far right has the speaker that would continue until the end of production in 1965. The four small holes were added to allow ventilation to the inside of the body.

Here we can see the changes made to Chatty Cathy's right hand. The doll on the left is from 1960-61, her first finger is pointing while the others are tightly curled. The two dolls on the right have fingers in a more "relaxed" posture. This was done for the new Chatty Cathy jewelry. Some jewelry sets had rings and bracelets while others had necklaces and barrettes.

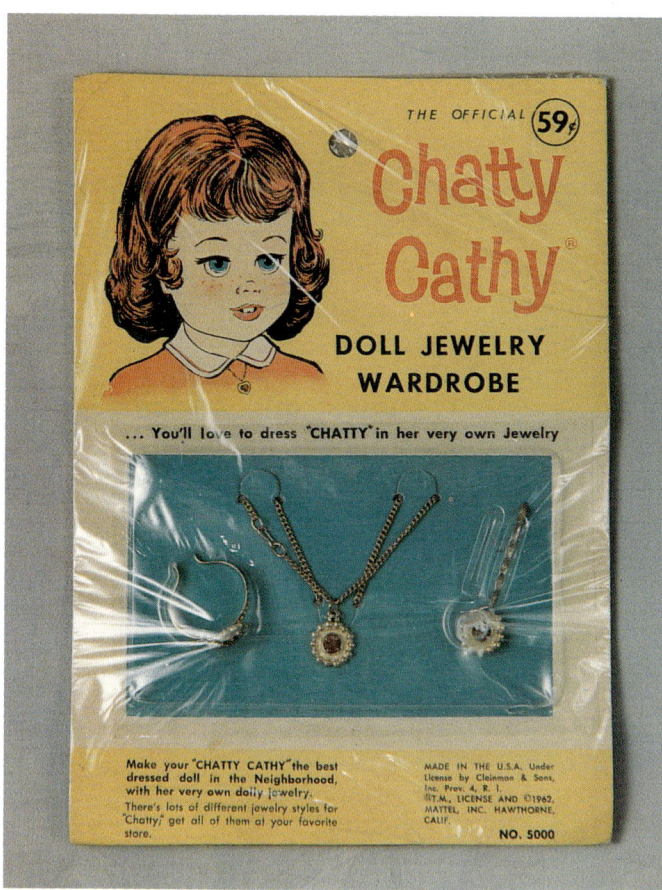

Chatty Cathy jewelry is one item that most people are unaware of. It was made by Cleinman and Sons of Rhode Island under license from Mattel. This jewelry is rare, and even more so when it's in the package. $100-150.

Black Chatty Cathy #0742 was 20" tall and introduced in 1962. She was made from the same molds as the white version. Her dress is the pink "Peppermint Stick". $600 and up.

Chatty Cathy Dress Patterns were made by the Advance Company for Mattel. Little girls who liked to sew could have fun making dresses for their Chatty Cathys. Patterns were also available for the later Chatty dolls. $15-25 each. $200-250 for entire display with patterns. *Photo by Sean Kettelkamp.*

Chatty Baby #0326, at 18" tall, was a delightful addition to Mattel's talking doll line in 1962. She's shown here with her original box and wrist tag. Her cute pixie haircut was also available in brunette. $175-200.

This is a Chatty Baby counter display. Displays such as this were sent out along with cartons of dolls, and department stores would display dolls on them. Counter displays were sent out also with Chatty Cathy and the later Chatty dolls. The Chatty Baby display seems to be the most common of these. Add $50 for display.

Chatty Baby's clothes were sold on display cards just like Chatty Cathy's. This one, Sleeper Set #0342, sometimes had a different variation of the rattle and pattern of the blanket. $40-50.

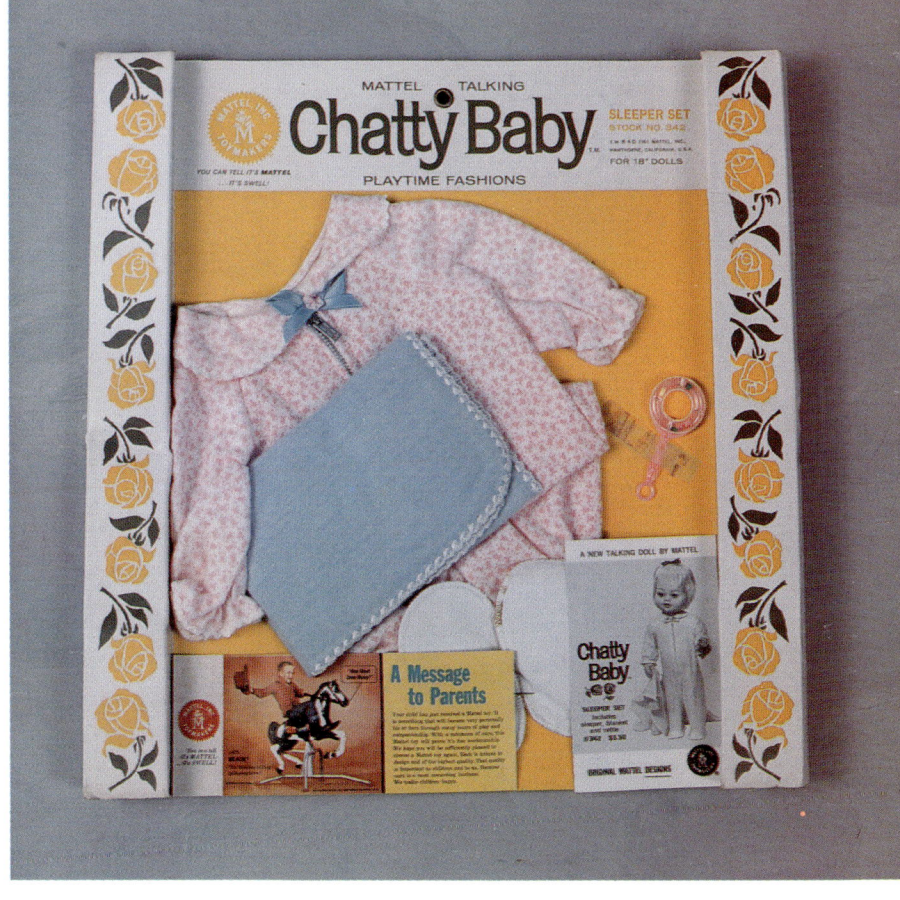

The same company that made all the Barbie doll cases made them for Chatty Baby too. She sat down inside and a small striped garment bag held her clothes. There were also small cardboard drawers to hold her shoes, hair ribbons, and rattles. The black Chatty Baby #0327 shown here was 18" tall and made from the same molds as the white version. Black Chatty Baby, $450 and up. Doll case, $50-75.

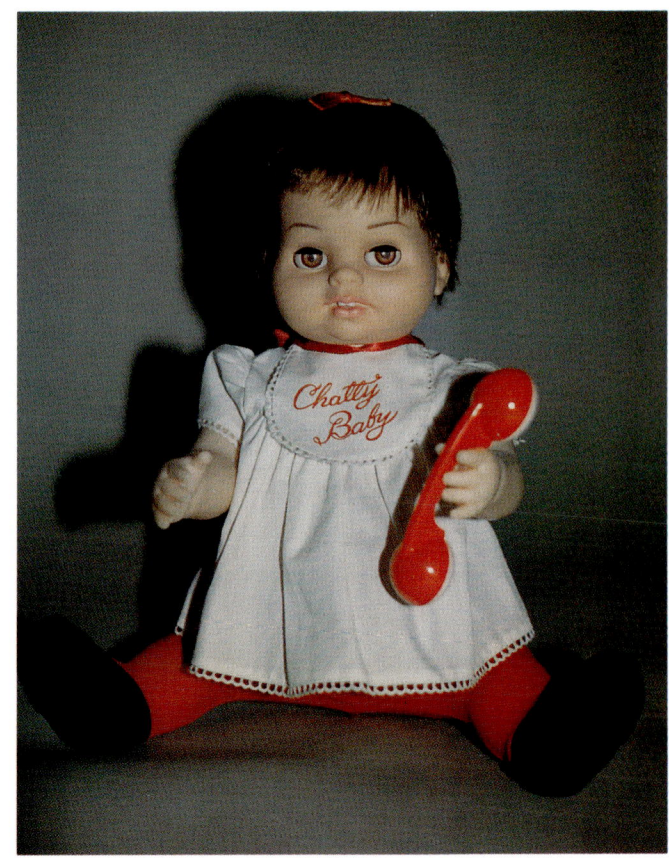

This Chatty Baby is considered rare because of her brown eyes. The outfit she is wearing is #0341, Leotard Set. It comes with a telephone rattle and the bib with her name is detachable. Brown eyed doll, $200 and up. Outfits, $40-50. *Courtesy Cyndie Steffen Collection. Photo by Cris Johnson.*

Chatty furniture became available in 1962. It was made by the Suzy Goose Toy Company, just like Barbie's. This Chatty Baby Pendulum Cradle could also be used for Chatty Cathy ... at least it said so on the box! The Suzy Goose Toy Company made other things too, like Chatty Cathy's Pencil Post Bed and Chifferobe. $175-200. *Courtesy Cyndie Steffen Collection. Photo by Cris Johnson.*

Here's the Chatty Play Table. It is very sturdy and made of metal; the removable orange seat is made of vinyl. $200-225. *Photo by Cris Johnson.*

Talking Beany Boy #0733, 17" tall, came straight from the favorite cartoon show *Beany and Cecil*. He was also available in a non-talking version; this one, however, says eleven different phrases. $275-300.

Beany Boy's head was made of plastisol, a durable and pliable type of vinyl. Chatty Cathy's head was made of the same material. This picture shows his "copter" nicely. It is tough to find a doll like this one, with the propeller not broken off.

Beany's pal in cartoon land was Cecil the Seasick Sea Serpent, #0735. He came in many different sizes, but only the large 18" one talked. He said eleven different phrases, many of them directed at Beany. $300 and up.

The Talk to Cecil Game was great fun for boys and girls. It came with a talking Cecil hand puppet, who, when the string was pulled, called out game moves. Little "Beany" game pieces were moved on a game board shaped like Cecil. It was from this game that the talking hand puppets were developed. $200-250.

D.J., or Dishonest John, was the villain on the Beany and Cecil cartoon show. He was always out to get Beany, who was always being saved by Cecil. One of D.J.'s phrases is, "I'll get that Beany Boy." $150-175.

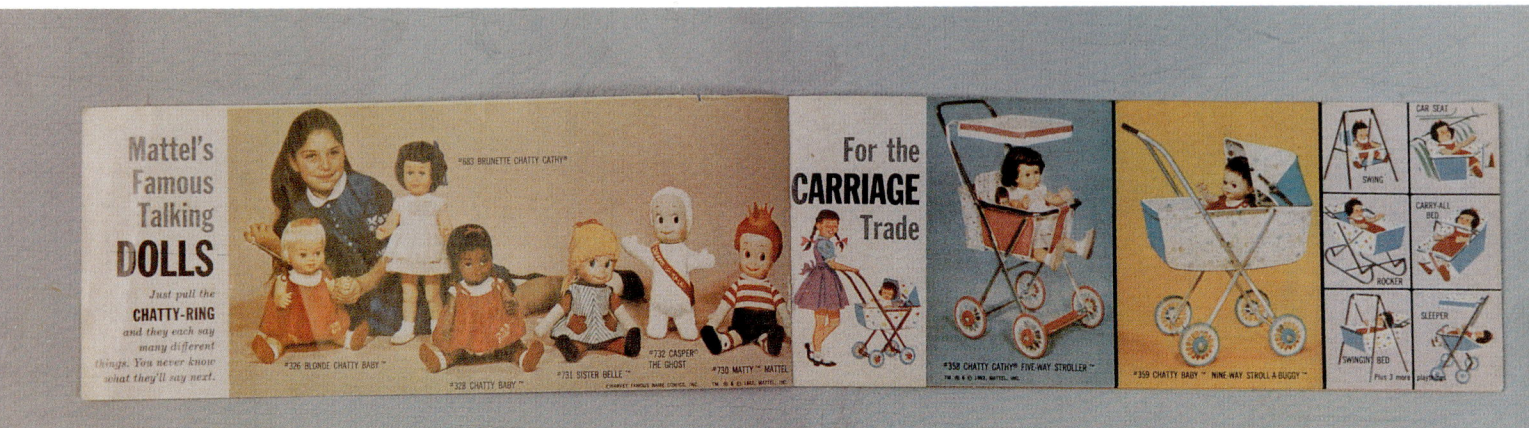

Inside this Mattel booklet one could see the dolls and other items that were available. The Chatty Stroller and Buggy were charming accouterments for the ever expanding Chatty world. $175-225.

Bugs Bunny #0743 was another doll inspired by cartoons. At 26.5" tall, he was the largest talking doll Mattel had made so far. Besides his size, he is distinguished by his vinyl hands. He was also the most popular among the talking stuffed toys. Bugs Bunny would be made in many different shapes and sizes over the next fifteen years. $200-225.

The cover of this Mattel booklet shows a real rarity. The little boy is riding Blaze, #415, the talking horse. In an age when little boys dreamed of being cowboys, this horse must have been fantastic! $150-200.

These black dolls are rare, because there were very few made. Besides 20" Chatty Cathy #0742 and 18" Chatty Baby #0327, 15" Tiny Chatty Baby #0272 was issued in 1963. Black Chatty Cathy, $600 and up. Black Chatty Baby, $450 and up. Black Tiny Chatty Baby, $450 and up.

Here is Chatty Cathy wearing her new "Party Dress" for 1962. This dress had been two-toned in 1960-61, but was all one vivid shade of royal blue in 1962. It was also sold separately!

Chapter 4 - 1963

Mattel Inc. Toy makers were riding a tidal wave of success in 1963. The Barbie doll was now wildly successful and Tiny Chatty Baby, Tiny Chatty Brother, and Charmin' Chatty were all ready to hit the stores. Barbie had undergone the first of many major makeovers. Her long ponytail had been transformed into the short, bushy bubble cut. Aware that changing their dolls' looks now and then to keep up with the times would also keep the public's attention, Mattel decided to change Chatty Cathy, even though she was still quite the rage.

As with Barbie, Chatty Cathy's body, limbs, and face remained the same and the most notable change was her hairstyle. Her hair was now available in a deep rich auburn as well as blonde or brunette, and was styled in long twin ponytails. Mattel toy catalogues from 1963 gushed, "The world's most famous doll ... more beautiful than ever!" The blue party dress was discontinued and replaced with a delightful dress of red "velvet" and white lace; she was also issued in the pink peppermint stick dress. Red Peppermint Stick #693 and Party Dress #691 had gone out of production in 1962. These were replaced in 1963 by two outfits that are the hardest to find today:
#398 "Sunny Day"
#399 "Sunday Visit"

All Chatty Cathy outfits had new packaging with cute little cartoon suns on them. Her box changed too, and had a full length color photograph of her standing on a French, red velvet tufted chair. Gift sets were another feature available in 1963. Now you could buy Chatty Cathy and Chatty Baby along with some of their outfits. This was the last year the black Chatty Cathy was on the market. Her hair was fashioned into the same long twin ponytails, but the Mattel catalogue states she is wearing a "red candy stripe dress." This may have been the discontinued red Peppermint Stick dress.

Another feature helped boost sales as well. The talking mechanism, now referred to as the "voice unit," was "new and improved." The speakers in all previous dolls had been made of paper, but were now made of a delicate, thin white plastic. This made her voice louder than ever before, *and* she said eighteen phrases instead of the previous eleven. Another interesting point was that the word "Chatty" had become a Mattel trademark, so now the child pulled the "Chatty ring" and "Chatty string," releasing it so the "Chatty record" inside the doll could play.

Like Chatty Cathy, Chatty Baby also said eighteen different phrases instead of eleven in 1963. The doll itself stayed the same and her packaging also remained unchanged, only the number of phrases listed on her box was altered. Two new outfits were added to Chatty Baby's existing wardrobe. They were:
#345 "Party Pink"
#348 "Outdoors"

The Casper the Ghost doll, originally issued in 1961 and made of terrycloth, was made of a plush white material in 1963. The stock number remained the same, and some Casper dolls had a removable red sash across the chest reading "Casper the Ghost." Others had "Casper" printed on the front of the doll in red.

Mattel followed similar marketing campaigns for both the Barbie and Chatty dolls, and licenses were sold to other companies to produce authentic "official" accessories for both dolls. Suzy Goose Toys, for example, made their furniture (bed, wardrobe closet, etc.) and the Whitman Paper Company printed paper dolls, coloring books, and puzzles.

Tiny Chatty Baby
Tiny Chatty Brother

These "Tiny" dolls created another splashy success for Mattel. Tiny Chatty Baby was simply a smaller 15" version of Chatty Baby that said eleven different phrases. Chatty Baby's face mold was scaled down so that both dolls actually had the same face, and both wore the same pixie haircut. Tiny Chatty Baby was available as a blonde or brunette, and a black version was issued as well. She was wearing an all-in-one aqua blue romper with her name on the bib, plus her matching aqua and white "slipper socks." Her box featured Tiny Chatty Baby's full color photograph, surrounded by Japanese origami bird and flower figures on an aqua background. The orange and black circle wrist tag was used, and she also had a wardrobe of four outfits available separately. Also marketed was a gift set containing the doll and three of these pretty outfits:
#281 "Bye-Bye"
#282 "Pink Frill"

#283 "Fun Time"
#284 "Nite-Nite"

Tiny Chatty Brother was the little boy of the Chatty group. He had the same body as Tiny Chatty Baby; they are virtually the same doll. One way to tell the two apart is by their hairstyle. Hers has a part at the crown of her head and is in a pixie style. His is parted on the side and combed over the top of his head. The other difference is his sweet voice that says eleven different phrases like, "Shake hands?" or "Hi dada!" There were no extra outfits available separately for Tiny Chatty Brother. He was issued in a darling all-in-one aqua blue shorts set with his name on it, along with "slipper socks" and a matching striped cap. His box has his picture on it, surrounded by drawings of a choo choo train, tug boat, helicopter, etc. He has the orange and black circle wrist tag. Since both dolls shared the same body mold, their mold mark looks like this:

```
TINY CHATTY BABY™
TINY CHATTY BROTHER™
©1962 MATTEL, INC.
HAWTHORNE, CALIF. USA
U.S. PAT. 3,017,187
OTHER U.S. AND FOREIGN
PATENTS PENDING
PATENTED IN CANADA 1962
```

Both dolls were also issued together in a wonderful gift set called Tiny Chatty Twins. They had a teeter-totter with yellow plastic seats connected with steel rods. This item is rare indeed today! The box has a full color photograph of the twins on it, and they are sitting on their teeter-totter in a park, with a tornado slide in the distance.

Charmin' Chatty

This clever cutie was touted by Mattel Inc. Toy makers as the doll who was "destined to make doll history." She was introduced at the American Toy Fair in New York City in March, 1963, and met with frenzied excitement. This Chatty doll didn't just talk...she talked and talked and *talked* when you pulled her string. Her secret was changeable records. She had a special voice unit that allowed tiny records to be easily put into, and removed from, a slot in her left side. The basic doll came with a set of five double-sided "Chatty records." Each changeable record had twelve phrases on each side. So with ten sides, Charmin' Chatty was able to speak 120 different phrases in all!

Her straight, shoulder length hair was available in blonde or auburn, and she stood 24" tall. She had vinyl arms, legs, and head. Her head was cocked to her right and she had an impish grin. She wore an outfit with a pretty navy blue skirt and a white middy blouse with a red sailor collar. She also wore red knee socks, blue and white saddle shoes, and a pair of cute plastic eyeglass frames. Her durable plastic body had a mold mark that looked like this:

```
CHARMIN CHATTY™
©1962 MATTEL, INC.
HAWTHORNE, CALIF. USA
U.S. PAT. 3,017,187
OTHER U.S. AND FOREIGN
PATENTS PENDING
PATENTED IN CANADA 1962
```

Charmin' Chatty was probably the most publicized of the early talking dolls. She was included in the World Book Encyclopedia's doll section, representing the quintessential modern doll of the era. She was also featured on the cover of the December 7, 1963 *Saturday Evening Post*. Inside, in an article written about new toys of the day, she is referred to as a "senior high school type doll." Actually she was made to resemble an American eight-year-old girl.

There was an extensive wardrobe available separately for Charmin Chatty. A special "Chatty record" was included with each outfit, so she could say phrases appropriate for each one. Mattel referred to her as "the doll that plays **with** you," and provided hats and other props with some of these sets for the child to wear. With the assortment of play and costume sets listed below, it was no wonder Charmin' Chatty was every little girl's perfect playmate!

Play sets:
#362 "Let's Play Cinderella"
#364 "Let's Play Tea Party"
#366 "Let's Talk 'n Travel in Foreign Lands"
#367 "Let's Play Nurse"
Costume sets:
#297 "Let's Play Birthday Party"
#298 "Let's Play Pajama Party"
#299 "Let's Play Together"
#300 "Let's Go Shopping"

The outfit #366, "Let's Talk 'N Travel in Foreign Lands", was a particularly unique one. It had four special "Chatty records" that allowed Charmin' Chatty to speak six foreign languages, as well as English with a British accent. The idea behind this playset was that Charmin' Chatty was going on an airplane trip around the world, and her owner was the stewardess! Included were a navy blue coat, red straw hat, shoes and socks, gloves, and a passport for the doll. The little girl had a stewardess cap, a "wings" pin, and a flight bag with the American Airlines logo stamped on it. There was also a foreign language folder so the child could learn and understand another language.

As with the other Chatty dolls, she was available in a gift set called "Charmin' Chatty Travels 'Round the World." It contained the basic doll and her five basic records, as well as all the contents of the outfit "Let's Talk 'N Travel in Foreign Lands." With the **nine** "Chatty records" in this gift set she could speak 216 different phrases in Spanish, French, German, Italian, Russian, Japanese, and English with a British accent.

Charmin' Chatty could also play games called "Chatty Games." Using the special "Chatty record" in each set, each child would take turns pulling the doll's string. Charmin' Chatty called out the moves, and one pull would be her "turn." Because you never knew what she would say next, she could actually win! There were two games in each box, four in all:
  #499 "Chatty at the Fair/Chatty Skate 'n Slide"
  #498 "Chatty Animal Friends/Chatty Animal Roundup"

Charmin' Chatty was accomplished and versatile, the perfect doll for any active little girl. Time hasn't faded her charm, and like her clothes-horse cousin Barbie, she is a prize for many doll collectors the world over.

Nearly everything in this picture is new for 1963. Chatty Cathy's box, wrist tag, dress, hair color, and hair style have been changed. Even her talking "voice unit" was updated and she could say eighteen phrases instead of eleven. The auburn hair was a new choice for the Barbie doll too. $250-300; Soft Faced Dolls, $300 and up.

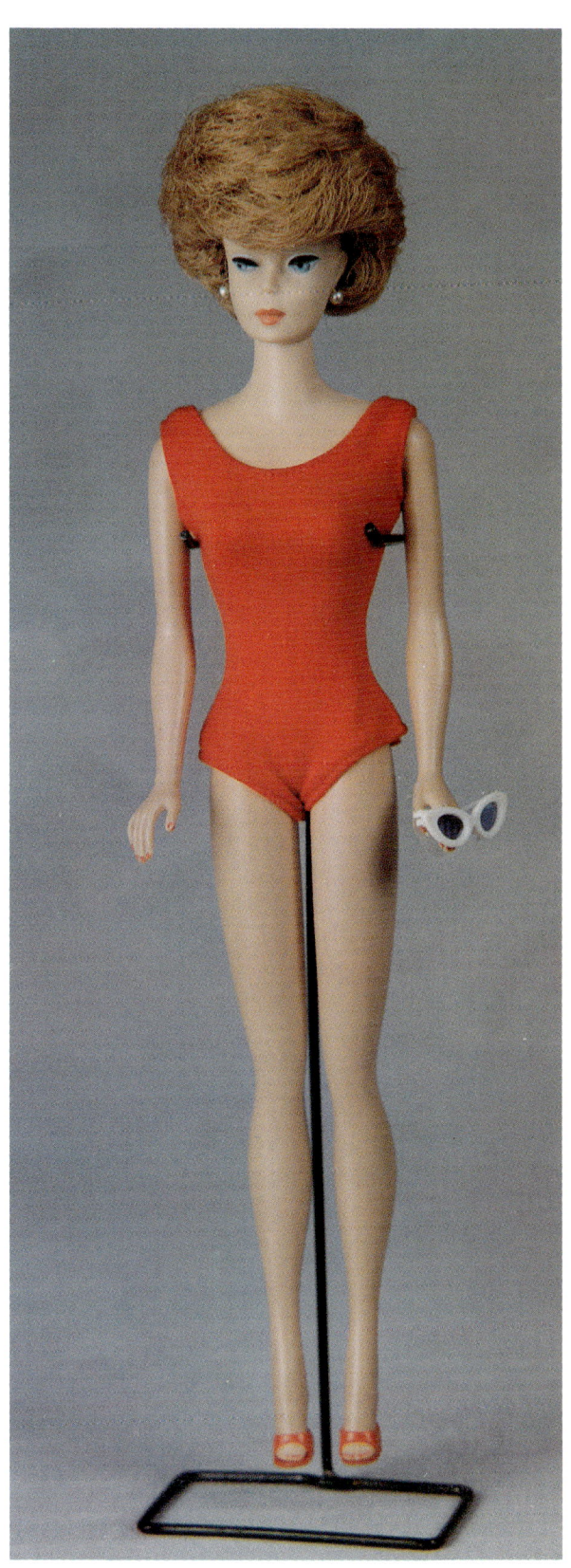

The Barbie doll got a major makeover late in 1962. Her ponytail is gone, and her new hairdo is referred to as a "bubble cut." By 1963, she was a firm favorite and her new red hair and swimsuit were winners! $600-700.

"Sunny Day" #398 was an outfit new for 1963. It was made of cotton and the colors were the rage of the early 1960s: aqua, orange, and acid green. $125 and up. *Photo by Chuck Klug.*

"Sunny Day" #398 Mint-in-Package. All Chatty Cathy outfits now had new packaging with cartoon "suns" along the border. $125 and up. *Photo by Sean Kettelkamp.*

"Sunday Visit" #399 had lovely shell pink shear nylon over a slightly deeper pink taffeta. Matching pink taffeta panties and taffeta shoes with white cotton socks completed the outfit. $125 and up. *Photo by Chuck Klug.*

Sunday Visit #399 Mint-in-Package. This was Chatty Cathy's most luxurious and detailed dress. It is considered rare. $125 and up. *Photo by Sean Kettelkamp.*

Chatty Baby Gift Set #329 included the doll and four of her outfits that were also available separately. Note that she is not wearing her "original" outfit. Most of the other gift sets for Chatty's included the outfit she was issued in as a single doll. Rare.

All Chatty outfits came to department stores in counter displays like this. Chatty Baby and Tiny Chatty Baby had their very own displays.

From 1962 to 1963 the only thing that changed on the Chatty Baby packaging was the number of phrases listed on the box.

This beautifully mint, soft-faced, pig tailed Chatty Cathy from 1963 is standing next to a 1960 first edition doll. Visually, the difference is immediately apparent. Mattel discontinued later edition soft-headed dolls in favor again of the harder, sturdier vinyl. The rooted hair in the squishy vinyl heads of later dolls tended to fall out easily when it was brushed! *Courtesy Cris Johnson Collection. Photo by Cris Johnson.*

This is a complete look at the black Chatty's of the 1960s. Note that the 1963 Chatty Cathy on the right has the new ponytail hairstyle. $850 and up. *Doll on far left, courtesy Ruth Kibbons Collection. Photo by Chuck Klug.*

Chatty Cathy gift set #396 included the doll with two outfits that were also sold separately. Note that her party coat and hat came with gloves; these gloves were not part of the outfit when it was sold separately. Rare.

In 1963, Chatty Baby got dressed-up in Party Pink #345 which was sold separately. It was a pretty dress that had pink sheer nylon over pink taffeta. Pink taffeta on white cotton slipper-socks and white cotton panties completed this outfit. $50-75. *Courtesy Cyndie Steffen Collection. Photo by Cris Johnson.*

Outdoors #348 was a companion outfit to complement #345 Party Pink. It was a rosy corduroy coat and matching head band. $100-150. *Courtesy Cyndie Steffen Collection. Photo by Cris Johnson.*

Casper the Ghost got an updated look in 1963. He was the same doll and said the same phrases but was now made of plush instead of terrycloth. The new packaging had a full color photograph of him on the front. $200-250.

This picture shows a variation of Casper the Ghost. Some of the dolls had the name Casper printed on the doll itself.

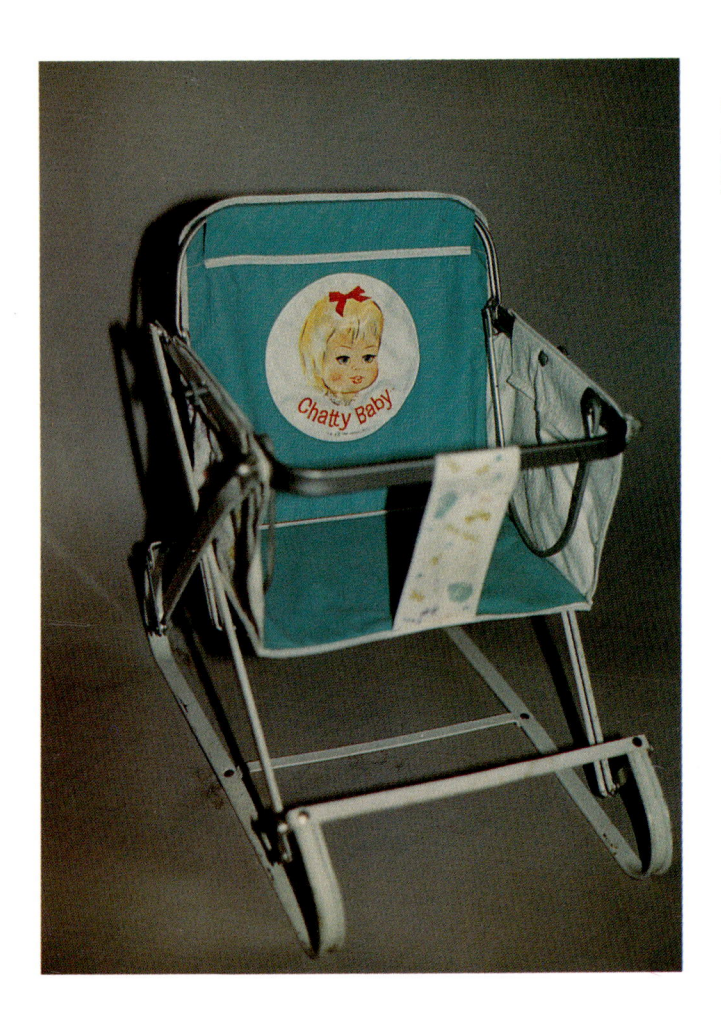

Chatty Baby's Nine Way Stroller could be taken apart and, as the name suggests, used in different ways. Here we see the Baby Swing part of the stroller, which could be down-sized to a car seat. $175-200. *Courtesy Cyndie Steffen Collection. Photo by Cris Johnson.*

The Chatty Baby Nursery Set was made by Mattel. The crib was a combination of cardboard sides and bottom with metal legs. The wardrobe closet was made of cardboard as well. This same cardboard construction was also used for many Barbie doll accessories, like Barbie's Dreamhouse. $150-175. *Photo by Sean Kettelkamp.*

This "Walk-n-Talk" stroller was made for both Chatty Cathy and Chatty Baby. A strap could be attached to their talking rings, so the strings could be pulled. While being walked, the dolls could then talk without being removed from the stroller ... clever! $175-200. *Courtesy Cyndie Steffen Collection. Photo by Cris Johnson.*

Whitman Paper Company printed paper dolls, coloring books, and similar items for the Chatty dolls—and for Barbie too!

Chatty Baby had many different paper products in her name too. Here are two types of coloring books, one with paper dolls included. A puzzle and a boxed set of paper dolls are also shown. $35-55 per item.

39

Chatty Cathy paper dolls had a cute 10" tall cardboard likeness of the doll, and many of her paper outfits looked just like their cloth counterparts. $40-50.

40

Tiny Chatty Baby #0270 was just a smaller 15" version of Chatty Baby. She had an adorable outfit, a cute pixie haircut, and she said eleven different phrases. The origami doves and flowers on her box were her symbols. They were also on her original outfit and accessory packaging. $200-250.

This Black Tiny Chatty Baby #0272 is 15" tall and wearing one of her original outfits that was also sold separately. #282 Pink Frill was a cute pink gingham dress covered with a layer of pink sheer nylon. A little blue appliqué added a nice touch on the bodice. Pink and white cotton gingham panties along with pink taffeta and white cotton slipper-socks completed the outfit. Note that her slipper-socks had pink taffeta ties at the ankle. $450 and up.

Tiny Chatty Baby's Gift Set #265 was another item in which the doll was sold with outfits usually sold separately. Not many Chatty gift sets were produced, but the Tiny Chatty Baby one is the most common. $300-350. *Courtesy Cris Johnson Collection. Photo by Cris Johnson.*

The cover art for the Chatty gift sets looked like Crayola sketches. Tiny Chatty Baby's packaging was pink, while Chatty Cathy's was green, and Chatty Baby's blue. *Courtesy Cris Johnson Collection. Photo by Cris Johnson.*

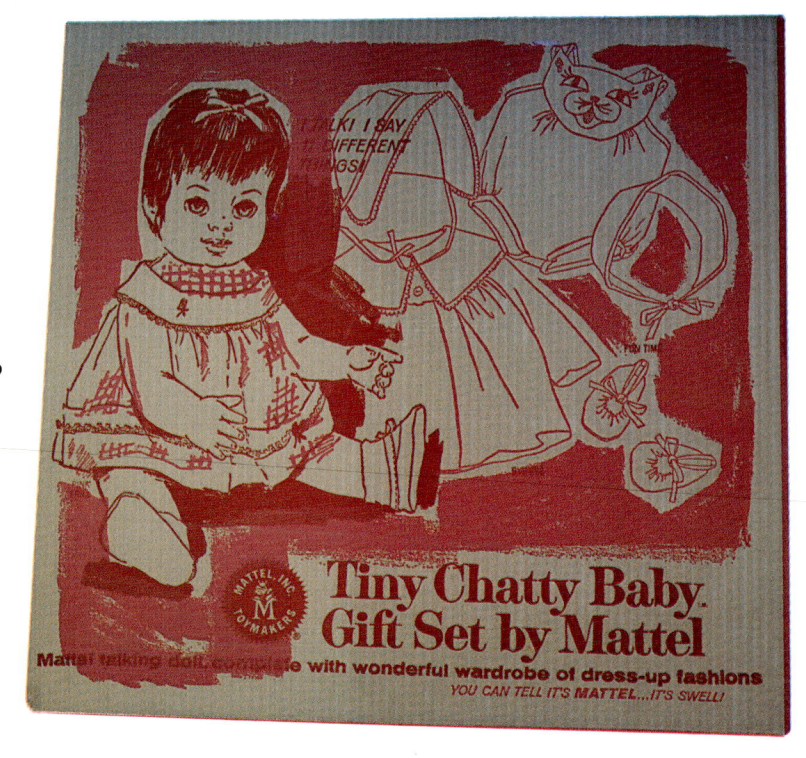

Packaging for Tiny Chatty Baby's clothes was like the other Chatty's. Simple display cards were used either in counter displays or hung on hooks. The artwork associated with Tiny Chatty Baby featured little doves and flowers. $60-75; Dash-n-Dots and Playmates outfits, $75 and up.

Tiny Chatty Baby had her own carrying case too! One side opened for the doll to stand in, the other side opened like a small "closet" for her wardrobe. It included a small cardboard drawer for her slipper socks and hair ribbons. $50-75 for the case only.

NEW!

CHATTY BABY NURSERY SET

CUSTOM-DESIGNED, EASY-TO-ASSEMBLE FURNITURE FOR ALL CHATTY BABY DOLLS.

#318   Retail: $6.00

Adorable three-piece nursery set of sturdy corrugated board, suitable for Chatty Baby, Tiny Chatty Baby™, or Tiny Chatty Brother™. Consists of matched crib, chair and 2-door wardrobe (with removable drawer, plastic hangers and hanger rod), all in dainty pink and blue design with a silhouette of Chatty Baby on the side. All three pieces come in compact segments, scored for easy assembly. Comes with plastic wardrobe door knobs and wooden white-tipped legs. Assembled sizes: wardrobe, 17-1/4" high x 13-1/2" wide x 6" deep; crib, 13-1/4" x 22" x 10"; chair, back height 10-1/2", seat 9" wide, 6-1/2" deep.

Std. Pack: 6/12 Doz.   Wt.: 40 Lbs.
Shipped from Garfield, New Jersey

This Mattel catalogue picture shows the Chatty Baby Nursery Set. It also explains that it could be used for Tiny Chatty Baby and Tiny Chatty Brother too!

Tiny Chatty Brother #0274, with his original box, outfit, and wrist tag. He stood 15" tall and did not have any other outfits available separately. He was only issued as a blonde. $200-250.

45

Tiny Chatty Baby and Tiny Chatty Brother were basically the same doll. The main differences were phrases and hairstyles ... and of course outfits. Tiny Chatty Baby's hair is a pixie cut, the hair brushes forward from the crown of her head. Tiny Chatty Brother's hair is parted on the side.

This side view of Tiny Chatty Brother shows the part in his hair nicely. His striped cap is sometimes hard to find, unless he is found Mint-in-Box.

The Tiny Chatty Brother on the left has a very soft squishy head, which actually makes the head larger. The doll on the right has a hard, rigid vinyl head. Another difference shown here is in the eyes. The doll on the left has "life-like decal eyes" while the one on the right has rarer "pinwheel eyes." Pinwheel eyes were used near the end of the production and substituted for the decal ones. Many collectors actually prefer the pinwheel version.

Tiny Chatty Baby #0270 and Tiny Chatty Brother #0274 teamed up as Tiny Chatty Twins #279-8 to make up this great gift set. They came with a teeter-totter that is very hard to find today. $500 and up. *Courtesy Cris Johnson Collection. Photo by Cris Johnson.*

Tiny Chatty Twins #279-8 was the only gift set to include Tiny Chatty Brother. Both dolls here are mint and each has the rare "pinwheel eyes." *Courtesy Cris Johnson Collection. Photo by Cris Johnson.*

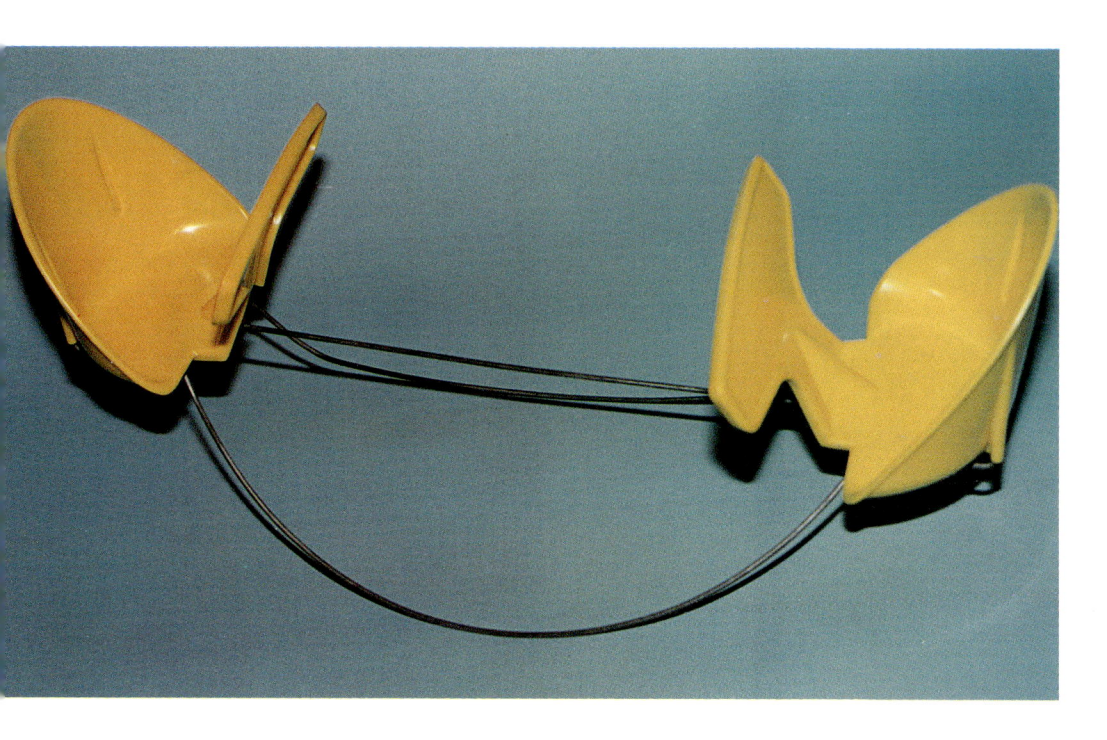

Here is a close-up view of the Tiny Chatty Twins teeter-totter. It is basically two yellow seats connected by steel rods, and is very rare. $150-200 for the teeter-totter only. *Courtesy Cris Johnson Collection. Photo by Cris Johnson.*

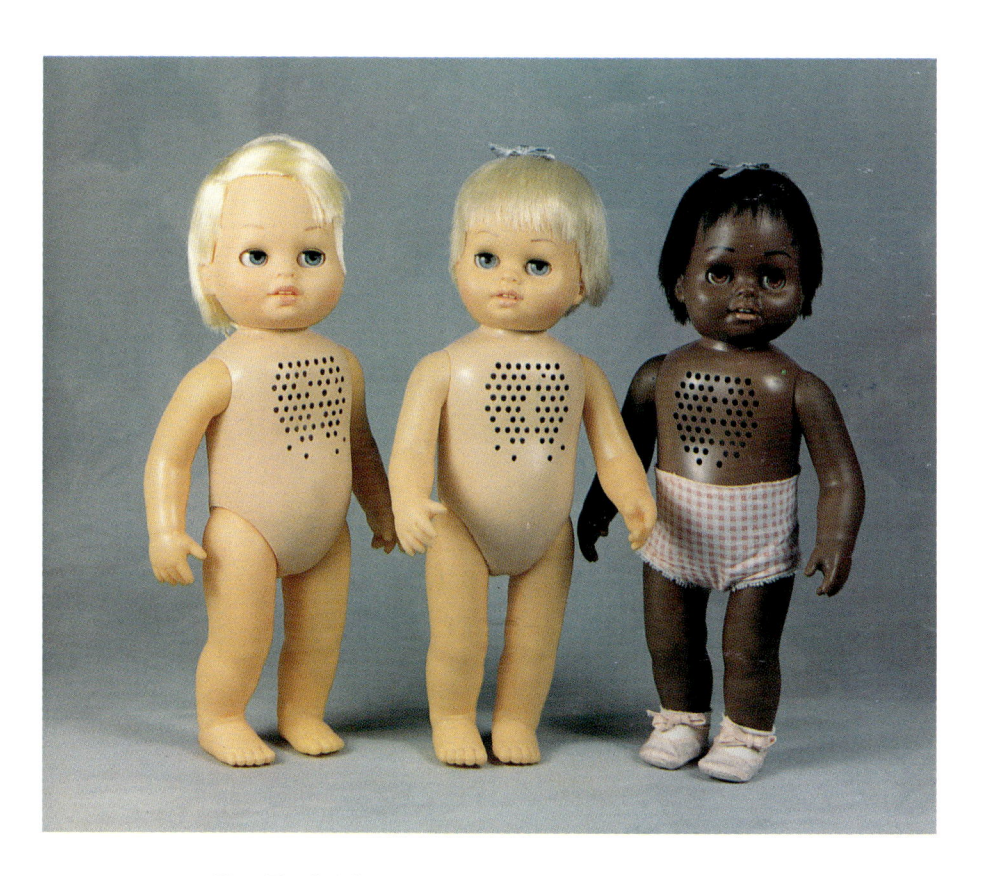

The "Tiny" dolls were all made from the same mold. Here is Tiny Chatty Brother #0274, Tiny Chatty Baby #0270, and Black Tiny Chatty Baby #0272. Each has the same speaker/grille and each has the same mold mark on the back.

49

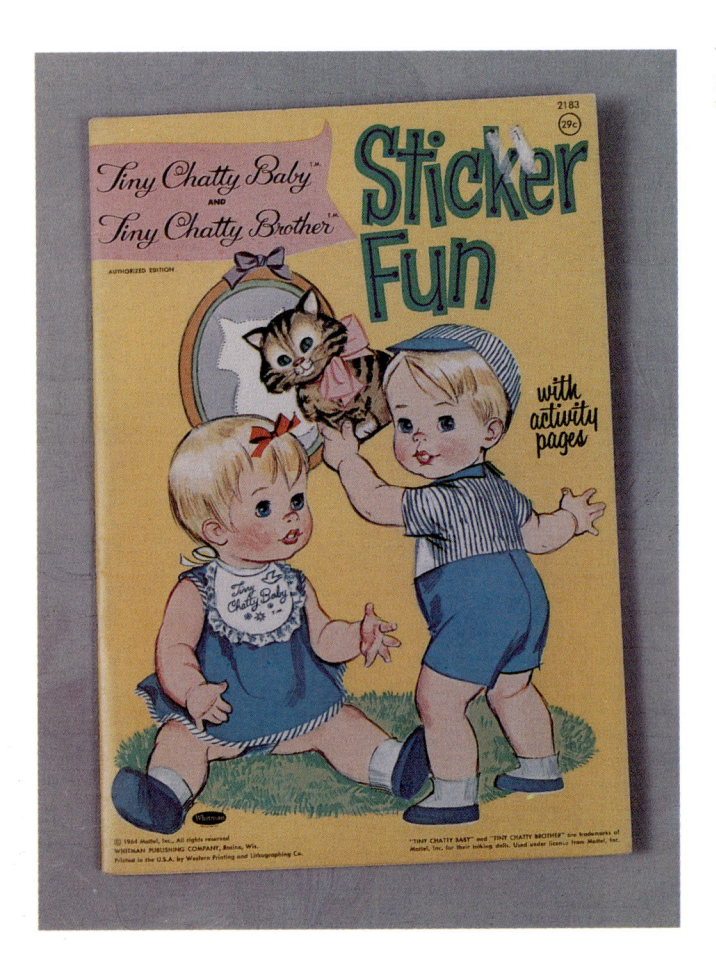

This is a Chatty Twins Sticker book. Many items such as coloring books, puzzles, and paper dolls were also made for them by the Whitman Paper Company. $40-50.

Inside the box with the Charmin' Chatty doll was her booklet and a package of four changeable records. Another record was already in the doll.

Charmin' Chatty #0292 was 24" tall and a sensational new addition to the talking doll line Mattel had established. The gimmick was changeable records. Now by changing the record, this doll could say hundreds of things. She is shown here with her original box, booklet, and four records (another record was already inside her). $250-300. Auburn hair is rarer.

Charmin' Chatty was issued as both blonde #0290 and auburn #0292. She was never issued as a brunette or in a black version.

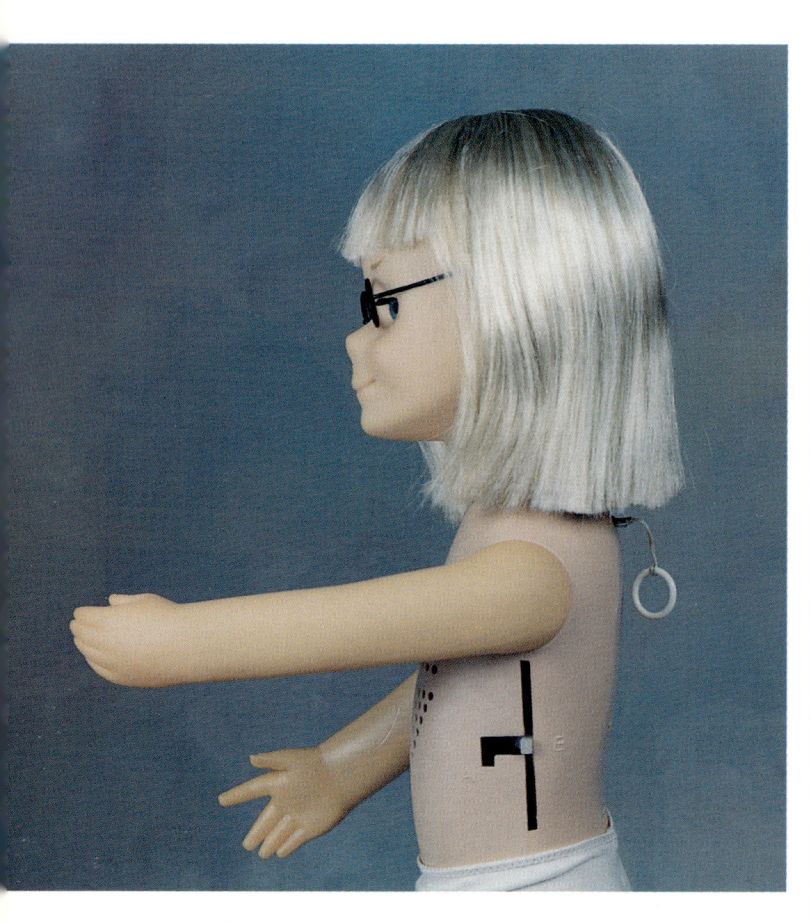

A slot on the left side of the doll made changing her record easy. When the lever was moved up and locked in place, the doll could be tipped and the record would roll out.

This view shows Charmin' Chatty's grille; it is the same for all. The position of the grille and its distance from the record slot is not far.

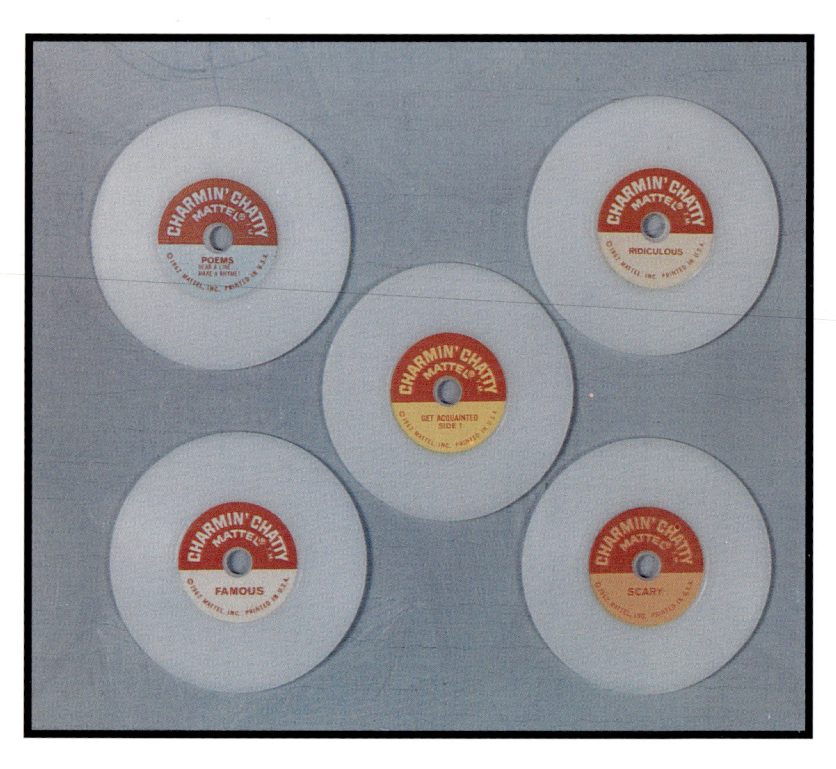

Here are the five basic Charmin' Chatty records. They were about 3" across and double-sided. Each record had twelve phrases on each side.

Here is the flip side of the five basic Charmin' Chatty records. The topics were usually (but not always) different on each side.

Here is a real rarity, a black Charmin' Chatty record. These were used when the doll first went into production. It was later found that they warped and didn't hold up well, especially in child's play. Very shortly after initial production, a white vinyl was used. Rare.

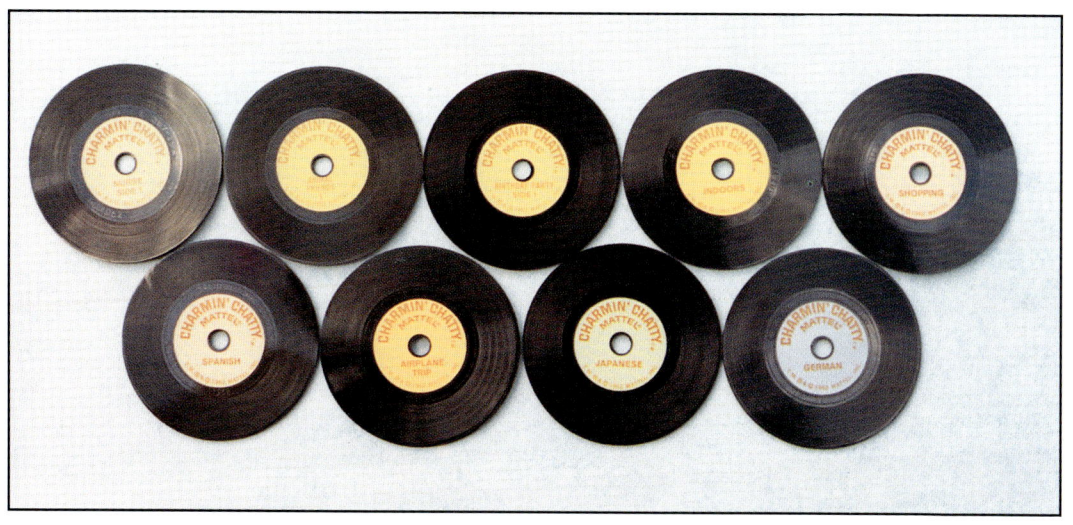

This group of black Charmin' Chatty records is quite unique, as they were not produced for very long. The "nurse" record in the upper left corner is slightly warped, as is the "shopping" record on the upper right. It was this flaw that led to the substitution of the white records. *Courtesy Cris Johnson Collection. Photo by Cris Johnson.*

Charmin' Chatty, like the other Chatty dolls, was issued with both hard vinyl and soft vinyl heads. The doll on the left has a hard vinyl head, which makes her head slightly smaller. Because of this, her hair looks a little longer and her bangs cover her eyebrows. The doll on the right has a soft vinyl head; as a result her head is slightly larger. Her cheek color is also not as vibrant because of the soft vinyl.

Charmin' Chatty could say hundreds of things and spoke seven different languages. Maybe it was because of these characteristics that she was featured on the cover of *The Saturday Evening Post*. Her name was mentioned in the toy article too. $40-50 for magazine.

This photo of Charmin' Chatty was in the *World Book Encyclopedia* for years. She was the quintessential modern doll of the era. All one needed to do was look up "doll" and her picture was featured in that article. Notice that the little girl is holding a black record!

Charmin' Chatty's saddle shoes were made in two different materials. On the left are a pair made of plastic; they have remained crisp white in spite of the years. The pair on the right are made of vinyl and are soft and pliable. The soft vinyl has yellowed and the blue of the "saddles" is a soft blue rather than navy. $20-30 per pair.

Barbie's little sister Skipper #950 was 9.25" tall. She had a best friend named Skooter #1040 who was the same size. Skooter, shown here, was a popular doll in her own right. Her face looks very much like Charmin' Chatty—could they have been crafted by the same artisans?

Charmin' Chatty's playsets were wonderful. Here is Let's Play Birthday Party #297, complete with hats, cake, candles, and invitation. Her dress is very much like Chatty Cathy's new original dress for 1963, but has tucks with lace inserts. It is also on the order of Barbie's "Silken Flame" #977 and Skippers Silk 'n Fancy #1902. The record included in this outfit is called Birthday Party, side 1 and 2. $100-125.

This outfit is called Let's Play Tea Party #364. Most Charmin' Chatty outfits came with "props" for the little girl. Here, she and the doll each get an apron to wear while preparing for their tea party! The record in the paper envelope is called Tea Party, side 1 and 2. $100-125.

For the outfit Let's Play Nurse #367, Charmin' Chatty is the patient and the child is the nurse. The doll wears the hospital gown, wrist band, and paper slippers. Each outfit had its own record; for this outfit she says phrases like, "I don't feel good." The record is Nurse, side 1 and 2. $100-125.

Here is the outfit Let's Talk 'N Travel in Foreign Lands #366. This is the most sought after outfit for Charmin' Chatty. She has a coat, straw hat, shoes, socks, red purse, and gloves. The little girl was the stewardess on an airplane trip around the world. This set had four records so the doll could speak German, Italian, French, Spanish, Russian, and Japanese. She also spoke phrases in a lilting British accent. The foreign language folder on the right helped the child pronounce the words! One record is called England, and the flip side is called Airplane Trip. The others are simply labeled by language. Note the American Airlines logo. Rare.

58

Let's Play Cinderella #362 came with two separate outfits, one for poor Cinderella, the other for rich Cinderella. In this set the little girl gets a "magic wand" and is the fairy godmother. The record for this outfit is Cinderella, side 1 and 2. On side 1 she is poor Cinderella and on side 2 she has been visited by her fairy godmother. $100-125.

Charmin' Chatty's outfit Let's Play Pajama Party #298, was a cute one. Here she has a nightgown, hair net, and slippers. There were also curlers and a brush and comb that little girls could use for themselves or the doll. $100-125.

This adorable outfit was called Let's Play Together #299. It was a rather simple outfit with tights that had attached shoes, and a smock with deep pockets. There was also a matching head scarf. The record for this outfit was called, appropriately, "Indoors and Outdoors". $125-150.

Let's Go Shopping #300 was Charmin' Chatty's least expensive outfit, yet very popular. It consisted of a skirt, short sleeve blouse, and matching crop top. The shoes and socks were part of her original sailor suit. The accompanying record is called Shopping on one side and Restaurant on the other. The shopping record is particularly cute because one phrase is, "Shall we buy a Barbie doll?" $125-150.

The ultimate gift set by Mattel was called "Charmin' Chatty Travels 'Round the World" #295. This is basically the Charmin' Chatty doll and the outfit, "Let's Talk 'N Travel in Foreign Lands" #366. The combined records, nine in all, included her five basic records and four foreign language records. They allowed her to speak 216 different phrases. Notice that all the stewardess items have the American Airlines logo on them! $800 and up.

Charmin' Chatty's outfits came packaged in frame trays and displayed the clothes nicely. The unusual thing here is that the outfit "Let's Talk 'N Travel in Foreign Lands" #366 came packaged in two frame trays. The artwork on the back of all Charmin' Chatty outfits packages is great! Notice the American Airlines logo.

Here is the artwork on the back of the two frame tray packages for Charmin' Chatty's outfit "Let's Talk 'N Travel in Foreign Lands". In at least one of the drawings Charmin' Chatty is portrayed as a brunette, yet no doll was ever produced as a brunette.

62

Chatty Games #498 and #499 were games that came with special Chatty Records. With the record placed in the doll, each child took turns pulling Charmin' Chatty's string. The doll would call out different moves and the child moved the small game pieces on the specially designed game board. Because one "turn" or pull of the string was for the doll, she could call out a move and win the game herself! The records were Animal Roundup, with the flip side Animal Friends, for one set, and At the Fair, with the flip side Skate 'n Slide, for the other set. $50-75.

Here are Charmin' Chatty's two puzzles. On the left is her "Birthday" puzzle and on the right her "Travel" puzzle. Both were made by the Whitman Paper Company in 1963 and 1964. $50-75.

Charmin' Chatty also had an array of paper products available separately. These included items like paper dolls, activity books, and story books. $50-75 per item.

63

Chapter 5 - 1964

During 1964 Mattel looked again to the cartoon world for inspiration. This time it was a popular television show called *The Funny Company*. The "sweetheart" of the show was a shy little girl call Shrinkin' Violette. The doll made to resemble her character was adorable, to say the very least. She was an all cotton rag doll with an over-stuffed head and yarn hair. Her talking voice unit was held firmly in place inside her head with foam rubber. Shrinkin' Violette also had the new "Yacker" feature, which meant that when you pulled her "Chatty ring" her mouth moved when she talked. She was extra special because her eyelashes fluttered as well. This was a great innovation, because now the toys could not only talk, they could be put into motion with the help of a new gear belt attached to their record.

Bozo the Clown was another cartoon character transformed into a talking doll in 1964. He was all plush with a vinyl head and said eleven different phrases. Mattel also came out with a doll called Baby Pattaburp. This was a non-talking doll that came with a baby bottle, and would burp when she was patted on the back. The black Chatty Baby was discontinued, and Tiny Chatty Baby got two new outfits for her existing wardrobe, called:
  #0286 "Playmates"
  #0266 "Dash 'n Dots"

In the talking toy department, "Animal Yackers" were introduced - their mouths moved when they talked. They were called Larry the Lion and Crackers the Parrot, and the secret to their success was that both boys and girls simply adored them.

Shrinkin' Violette #5383, 12" in the sitting position, was a doll inspired by the cartoon T.V. show, *The Funny Company*. She was all stuffed cotton and had her talking "voice unit" inside her head. The voice unit was also attached to her eyes and mouth with a small cable. When her "Chatty ring" was pulled, her eyelashes would flutter and her mouth would move as she talked. She could say eleven different phrases. They were usually something shy, such as, "I have butterflies in my tummy." $250-300.

Even soft bodied dolls like Shrinkin' Violette #5383 had paper doll counterparts. These were made by Whitman Paper Company. $40-50.

Bozo the Clown #0314, was 18" tall and had a stuffed body. Only his blue and white spotted outfit was removable. He spoke phrases like "Whoaaa Nellie!" in his original T.V. voice, provided by Bozo creator Larry Harmon. $150-175.

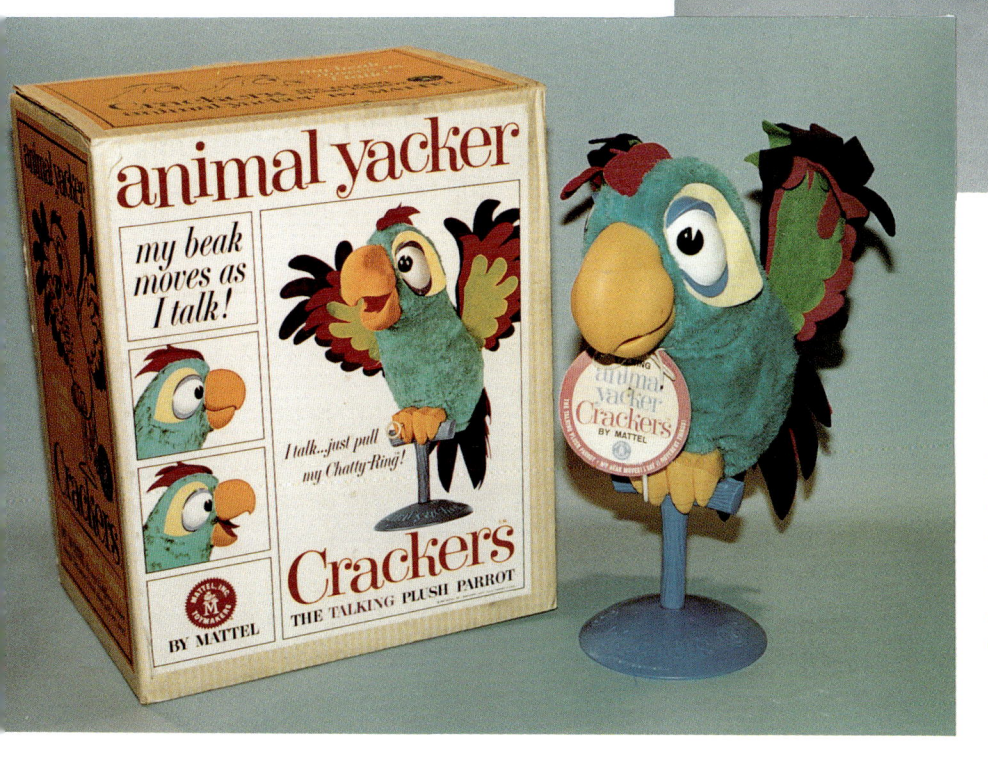

Crackers the Parrot #0381, was 15.5" on his perch and was one of the toys called an "Animal Yacker." Like Shrinkin' Violette, a cable was attached to the record inside. When the "Chatty Ring" was pulled, Crackers' mouth moved as he talked. He would say things like, "My grandfather was an eagle." There was also an Animal Yacker called Larry the Lion #0381. $250-300. *Courtesy Michael Izzo Collection. Photo by Cris Johnson.*

Chapter 6 - 1965

Mattel brought forth a flood of imaginative, original designs for some of the new talking dolls and toys in 1965; a few, of course, were still modeled after cartoon characters. The soft body designs were used more and more due to their versatility, and because they were cuddly and more soft than ever before. The dolls introduced were:

    #3055 Singin' Chatty
    #3035 Baby First Step (non-talking)
    #3033 Dee-Dee (non-talking)
    #3040 Baby Cheryl
    #3091 Drowsy
    #3092 Baby Colleen (Sears Exclusive)
    #5314 Scooba Doo
    #5320 Tatters
    #5317 T-Bone
    #5318 Porky Pig
    #5313 Woody Woodpecker
    #5316 Herman Munster
    #5312 Bugs Bunny
    #5385 Chester O'Chimp

Mattel took a side step from their talking doll phenomenon long enough to introduce non-talking Baby First Step. She was battery operated, and touted as the world's first *walking* doll. As years went by her popularity soared and she went through many transformations. Dee Dee was another non-talking doll who made her debut in 1965. She came with different costumes and outfits that were put together with a Mattel method of non-sewing called "Cut 'n Button." Some of these Cut 'n Button outfits were available separately for different members of the Barbie doll family too. Continuing her evolution, Barbie now sported her new "American Girl" hairstyle and bendable legs.

Mattel expanded its talking toy line in another unique way. Cartoon and television characters available as dolls were now issued as talking hand puppets as well. Cloth puppet bodies were attached to scaled down heads that looked identical to their doll counterparts:

    #5378 Herman Munster
    #5370 Porky Pig
    #0376 Bugs Bunny
    #5379 Bozo the Clown
    #5374 Woody Woodpecker
    #0377 Mr. Ed, television's talking horse (not available in doll version)

These puppets were very popular. The dolls and talking hand puppets very often had the same voice unit and said the same phrases.

Singin' Chatty

In 1965, Mattel distributed a little vocalist to department stores and created yet another sensation. She was called Singin' Chatty. She stood 17" tall and had a durable plastic body with vinyl arms, legs, and head. Her hair was cut in a collar length bob, feathered at the sides. Long bangs were swept across her forehead and secured at the side with a perky red ribbon. She was available as a blonde or brunette, and had a new kind of blue sleep eyes with long curly eyelashes. These were the same eyes used for Baby First Step. Singin' Chatty was the last doll of the 1960s to have the word "Chatty" incorporated into her name. She was in department stores from 1965 to 1966, received "bravos" in toy departments, and sold very well. Sears department stores brought her back for an "encore" in 1967.

The body style and mold used for Singin' Chatty was the same one used for Tiny Chatty Baby and Tiny Chatty Brother. In fact, the very first issue of Singin' Chatty had a mold mark that looked like this:

```
SINGIN' CHATTY™
TINY CHATTY BABY™
TINY CHATTY BROTHER™
©1962 MATTEL
HAWTHORNE, CALIF. USA
U.S. PAT 3,017,187
OTHER U.S. AND FOREIGN
PATENTS PENDING
PATENTED IN CANADA 1962
```

Some of these very early dolls had a slightly different hairstyle that had short straight bangs. They also had some very uncommon *green* eyes, and freckles on their cheeks. Shortly afterward a slight change was made to the body mold. The neck stem was made slightly longer, so that over the next twenty years it would easily fit new head designs. Along with this came a new mold mark:

```
SINGIN' CHATTY™
©1964 MATTEL, INC.
HAWTHORNE, CALIF. USA
PATENTED IN USA
PATENTED IN CANADA 1962
OTHER PATENTS PENDING
```

Singin' Chatty did not have any clothes available separately, but the outfit she was issued in was adorable and of fine quality. She came wearing a red dress with white musical notes printed across the skirt; some skirts had the name "Singin' Chatty" printed on them too. Two different collar styles were used: the earlier dress had a plain tab collar with a narrow white band beneath the bodice; the later one still had the white band at the bodice but also had a little bib attached to the collar with two tiny pearl buttons and a tiny red bow. She also wore red cotton panties with white edging around the legs, white socks, and red shiny "patent leather" T-strap shoes to complete her outfit.

Singin' Chatty sang long phrases of children's classics, like "Old MacDonald had a Farm," "The Farmer in the Dell," and "Twinkle, Twinkle Little Star," all in a cute little girl's voice.

As the talking doll craze forged ahead to new heights, Mattel very quietly and without fanfare discontinued Chatty Cathy.

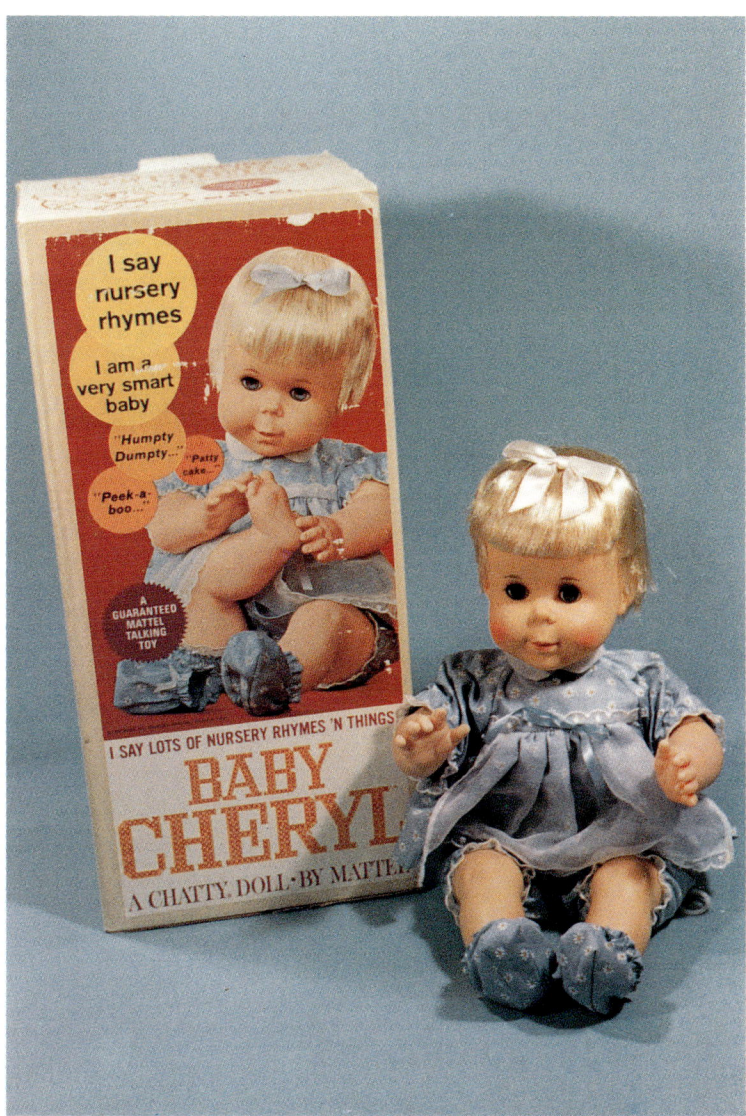

Baby Cheryl #3040, 16" tall, was a "Chatty" doll of a different sort. Her body held the voice unit, and it was surrounded by foam stuffing covered with cloth. Her vinyl head, arms, and legs were sewn onto her cloth body. She said eleven different babyish phrases. $175-200. *Courtesy Michael Izzo Collection. Photo by Cris Johnson.*

Baby First Step #3035 was 18" tall and issued in 1965. She was a non-talking doll touted as the world's first walking doll. Over the years she went through many transformations. This is a first edition. $75-100. *Courtesy Carmen Tickle Collection. Photo by Cris Johnson.*

Tatters #5320, was a 19" tall rag doll who said eleven different phrases about her "rags." She is made of all cotton cloth construction. Much of her facial expression is printed on the cloth. She is hard to find complete with her safety pin and head scarf. $150-175. *Courtesy Michael Izzo Collection. Photo by Cris Johnson.*

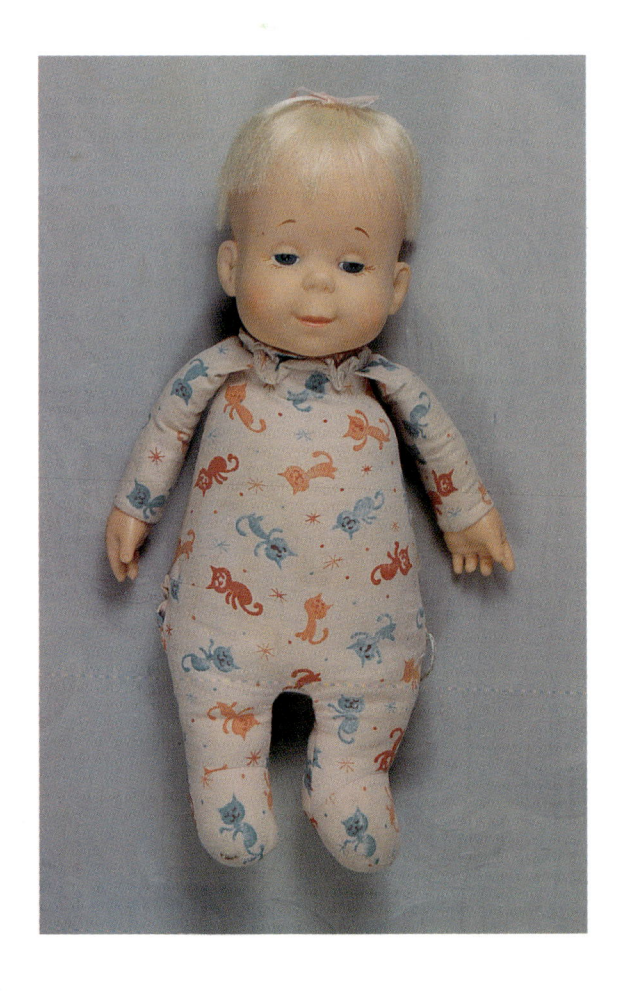

Scooba-doo #5314 was a beatnik! She had long legs and was 23" tall. Her hair was available in blonde #5315 or brunette. Today, she's hard to find with her striped shift dress and gold necklace. $275-300. *Courtesy Cris Johnson Collection. Photo by Cris Johnson.*

Drowsy #3091 was an adorable 15.5" talking doll. As her name and "kitty" pajamas suggest, she's ready to go to bed. She says eleven sleepy phrases and was available for many years. After two years her pajamas were changed to bright pink flannel with white dots. That is the way many collectors find her today...the "kitty" pajamas are more rare. $125-150.

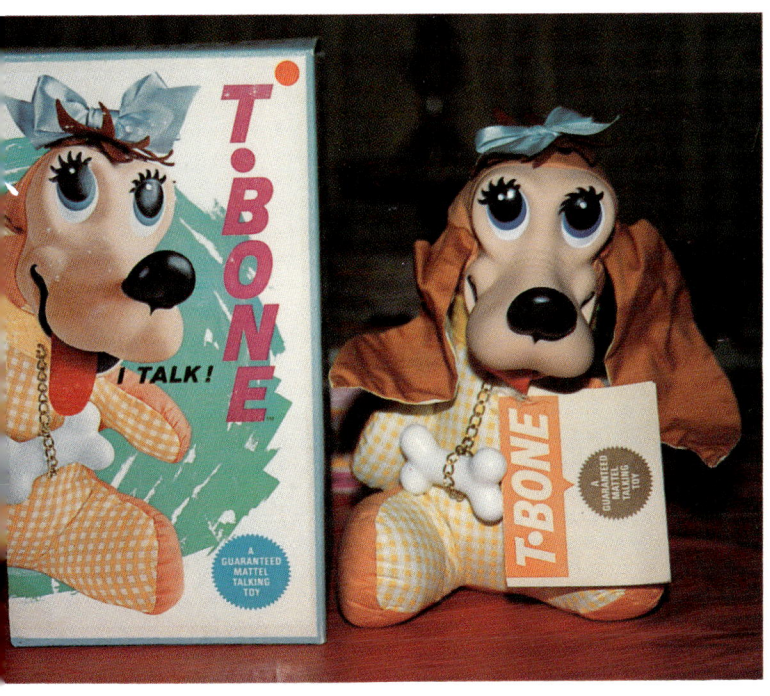

Here is T-Bone #5317, Mattel's Southern belle. She's 11" tall while sitting and says eleven different phrases. The cotton cloth construction includes a molded vinyl face, collar, and chain. Don't let her hound dog looks and bone fool you. One of her phrases—in a southern drawl—was, "Ah'm not very smaht, but Ah'm cheerful." $200-250. Courtesy Michael Izzo Collection. Photo by Michael Izzo.

Porky Pig #5318, was 17" tall and said eleven different phrases in his cartoon voice. He has a vinyl head sewn on a stuffed body. His striped jacket and bow tie are removable. $150-175. Courtesy Michael Izzo Collection. Photo by Cris Johnson.

Herman Munster #5316 was 21" tall and was based on the character from the T.V. show *The Munsters*. His Frankenstein type looks consisted of a green vinyl head and hands. The rest of his body was blue corduroy and black cotton. He said eleven different phrases in his T.V. voice provided by actor Fred Gwynne. $300-350.

Bugs Bunny #5312 was modified in 1965. He was shortened a bit from 26.5" to 24" tall. His vinyl hands were replaced by furry paws, but he still has a carrot glued in place. Even though he was scaled down, the phrases stayed the same. This particular doll was available for almost ten years. $100-125.

Here is Bugs Bunny past, present, and future. The doll on the left is the first edition, next to him is the scaled down version from 1965. The Bugs Bunny puppet was also issued in 1965. The smaller 11" version is from 1971. The all plastic "Chatter Chum" is from 1977 and his mouth opens and closes as he talks. Many of them say the same phrases. $50-75 for the Chatter Chum only.

Chester O'Chimp #5385, was 14" tall and the third Animal Yacker available. His mouth moved as he talked, and he spoke with an Irish brogue. He would say things like, "Let's go to the zoo and see the wild children." His vest is removable. $175-200. *Photo by Chuck Klug.*

Talking hand puppets were fun additions to the talking toy line. Cartoon and T.V. characters that were available as dolls were also issued as puppets. This Woody Woodpecker puppet #5374, said the same phrases as the doll counterpart. The talking voice unit was sewn inside the puppet's "mitten", and the child just pulled the "Chatty ring" to hear the voice. $150-175. *Courtesy Michael Izzo Collection. Photo by Cris Johnson.*

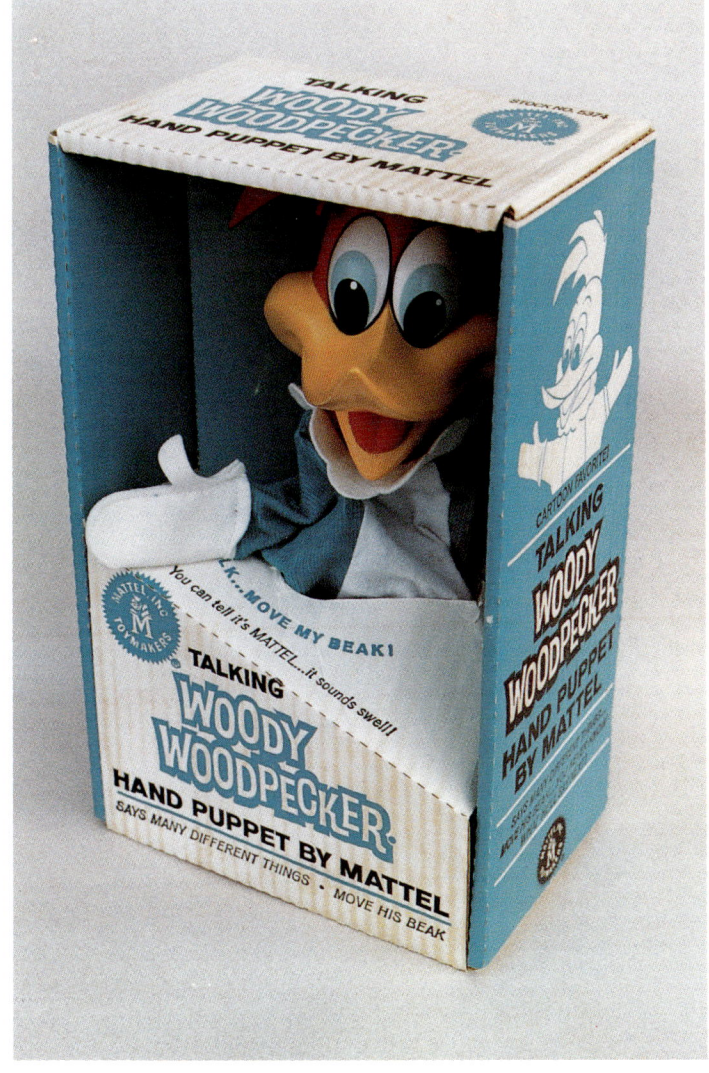

Mr. Ed #0377, was a favorite puppet for boys and girls. He said eleven different phrases in his original T.V. voice. This puppet did not have a doll counterpart. $150-175. *Courtesy Michael Izzo Collection. Photo by Cris Johnson.*

The puppets are hard to find M.I.B. There were also puppets for Herman Munster, Porky Pig, and Bugs Bunny. $150-175; Herman Munster, $175-225. *Courtesy Michael Izzo Collection. Photo by Michael Izzo.*

Singin' Chatty #3055 was 17" tall and the last doll of the 1960s to have the word "Chatty" incorporated into her name. She was very basic, and no wardrobe was issued separately for her. She sang long phrases of children's classics when her "Chatty ring" was pulled, such as, "Row, row, row your boat … life is but a dream." Her box also had a plastic wrapping. $200-250. *Courtesy Cris Johnson Collection. Photo by Cris Johnson.*

Here is a Bozo the Clown #0314, with an unusual hand puppet. Most puppets had the same blue and white dotted material. This plain blue version may be a Sears exclusive. $150-175 for the hand puppet only.

Singin' Chatty was 17" tall and available as blonde #3055 or brunette #3066. Her dress had a variety of different styles; some had her name spelled out between the musical notes. The most common dress variation was to the collar and bodice. The body mold was the same one used for Tiny Chatty Baby and Tiny Chatty Brother; only the neck was slightly altered. $200-250. *Courtesy Cris Johnson Collection. Photo by Cris Johnson.*

Singin' Chatty #3055 was an adorable doll. Notice the high cheek color. Her dress has the variation collar/bodice, but the panties are original ... red cotton with white edging. $200-250. *Courtesy Cris Johnson Collection. Photo by Cris Johnson.*

The back of the Singin' Chatty box had a hole where her string could be pulled without removing her from the box. This was a new feature used on many boxes afterward. Notice the hairstyle and freckles in the illustration of the doll. Singin' Chattys with bangs and freckles are first issue and are somewhat more rare, but they do exist! Very often these first edition dolls had the names Tiny Chatty Baby and Tiny Chatty Brother included in the mold mark. *Courtesy Cris Johnson Collection. Photo by Cris Johnson.*

As 1965 came to a close, Chatty Cathy was discontinued. Many of her different shoes are shown here; they are all original. Toward the end of production in 1965, the shoes were nothing more than flocked cardboard (bottom right). Red, pink, turquoise shoes, $25-35. Shoes with Glen Plaid lining (not shown), $40-50.

Here is an "American Girl" Barbie in a new outfit for 1966, #1668 "Riding in the Park." $500.

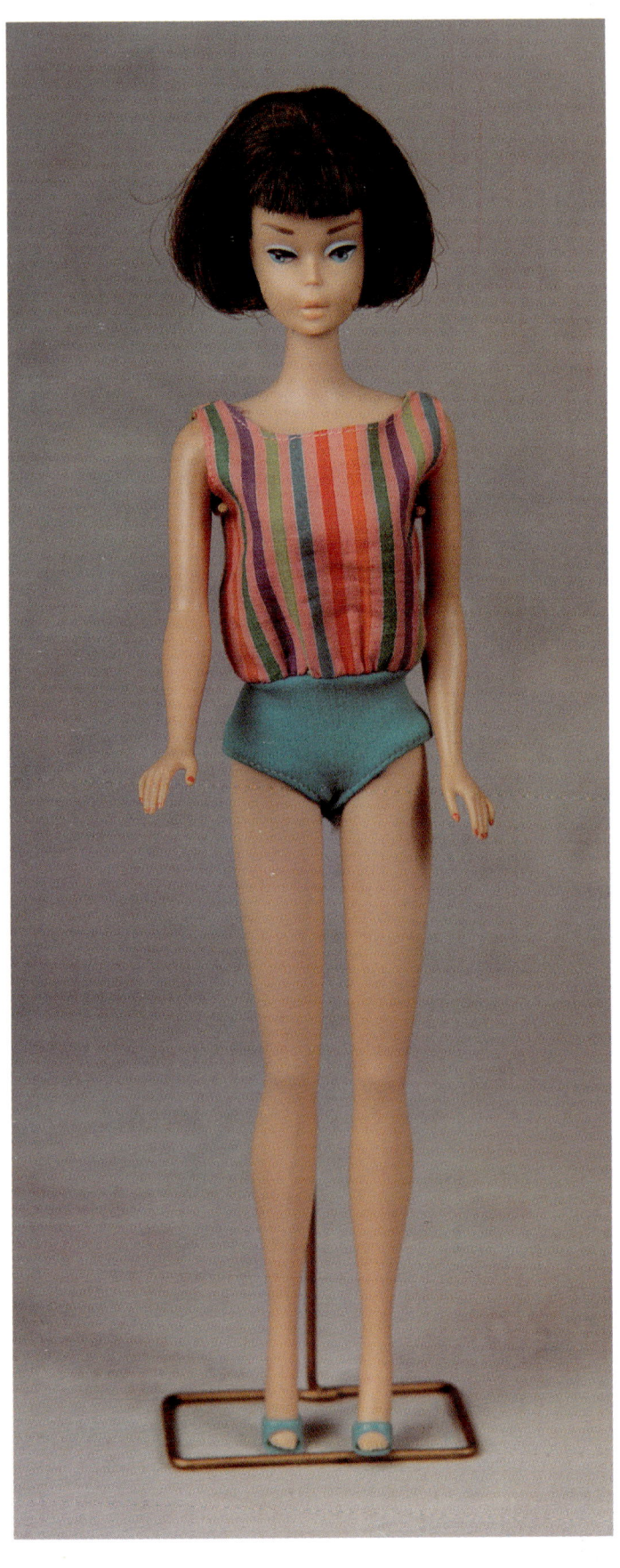

Barbie got another makeover in 1965. Her hair was styled in a "bob" and she got a fantastic new striped bathing suit. For the first time her legs were bendable. This doll is known to collectors as an "American Girl." $1200-1500.

Chapter 7 - 1966

1966 was another great year for Mattel. It was the year that Barbie got Color Magic Hair and a new doll line was introduced called Liddle Kiddles. Chatty Cathy was gone, but so many wonderful talking dolls and toys were being distributed that no one seemed to notice. All the talking dolls issued in 1966 had the soft body design. Some non-talking dolls were introduced too, each making their own delightful impact on the toy industry. These dolls were new for 1966:

- #3096 Baby Teenie Talk
- #3041 Baby Secret
- #3036 Cheerful Tearful (non-talking)
- #3094 Tiny Baby Pattaburp (non-talking)
- #3097 Teachy Keen (Sears exclusive)
- #3037 Baby Step (Sears exclusive)
- #5322 Pattootie
- #5321 Tom & Jerry
- #5390 Biff the Bear
- #5319 Linus the Lionhearted
- #0314 Bozo the Clown (same doll - now Sears exclusive)
- #5384 Bernie Bernard (Animal Yacker)

Talking Hand Puppets - 1966
- #5371 Linus the Lionhearted
- #5380 Tom & Jerry
- #5366 Popeye (Sears exclusive)
- #5378 Herman Munster
- #5370 Porky Pig
- #0376 Bugs Bunny
- #0377 Mr. Ed

Woody Woodpecker and Bozo the Clown hand puppets were now discontinued, only to be brought back later as Sears exclusives.

Baby Secret #3041 had a soft vinyl head like Baby Teenie Talk #3096, and was 18" tall. When her string was pulled her mouth moved as she "whispered" rather loudly. The "Yacker" voice unit was used to move her mouth, and she said eleven different "secrets." $100-125.

Baby Teenie Talk #3096 was new for 1966 and a new type of doll for Mattel. She was 17" tall and her head was made of very soft, pliable vinyl. The talking "Yacker" voice unit used for the Animal Yackers was used here and attached to the inside of her mouth. When her string was pulled her mouth moved as she spoke one of eleven babyish phrases. Her outfit is original. $150-175.

This picture is from a 1967 Sears Roebuck Christmas Wish Book. "Baby Step" #3037 was a Sears exclusive by Mattel in 1966 and was available for two years. She is simply "Baby First Step" with a redesigned hairstyle and outfit. *Courtesy Cris Johnson Collection. Photo by Cris Johnson.*

Teachy Keen #3097 was a little teacher. When her string was pulled she would say things about grooming, counting, or telling time. She was 16" tall and came with several props so the child could have fun learning. Phrases included "Comb my hair" and "Buckle my shoes." $100-125. *Courtesy Michael Izzo Collection. Photo by Cris Johnson.*

This ad was featured in *LIFE* Magazine in 1966. The individual photos together create an adorable menagerie of Mattel toys. Larry the Lion #3071 in the bottom left picture was one of the original Animal Yackers from 1964; he was on the market for almost ten years! *Photo by Cris Johnson.*

Pattootie #5322 was a cute clown doll and stood 16" tall. He was a performer that used his box as a "stage." He was wearing a mask to make a sad face, many of his eleven phrases had sound effects too. His harlequin suit and collar are removable. $250-300. Courtesy Michael Izzo Collection. Photo by Michael Izzo.

Here is Pattootie #5322 without his mask. The head and body construction is much like Drowsy #3091 from 1965. Underneath the suit his body is red cotton.

Linus the Lionhearted #5319 was 21" tall and from a Saturday morning cartoon show of the same name. He was very popular and was also issued as a talking hand puppet. $125-150. Courtesy Michael Izzo Collection. Photo by Cris Johnson.

Linus the Lionhearted Puppet #5371 was one of nine talking hand puppets available in 1966. He says the same eleven phrases that the talking doll says. $100-125. *Courtesy Michael Izzo Collection. Photo by Cris Johnson.*

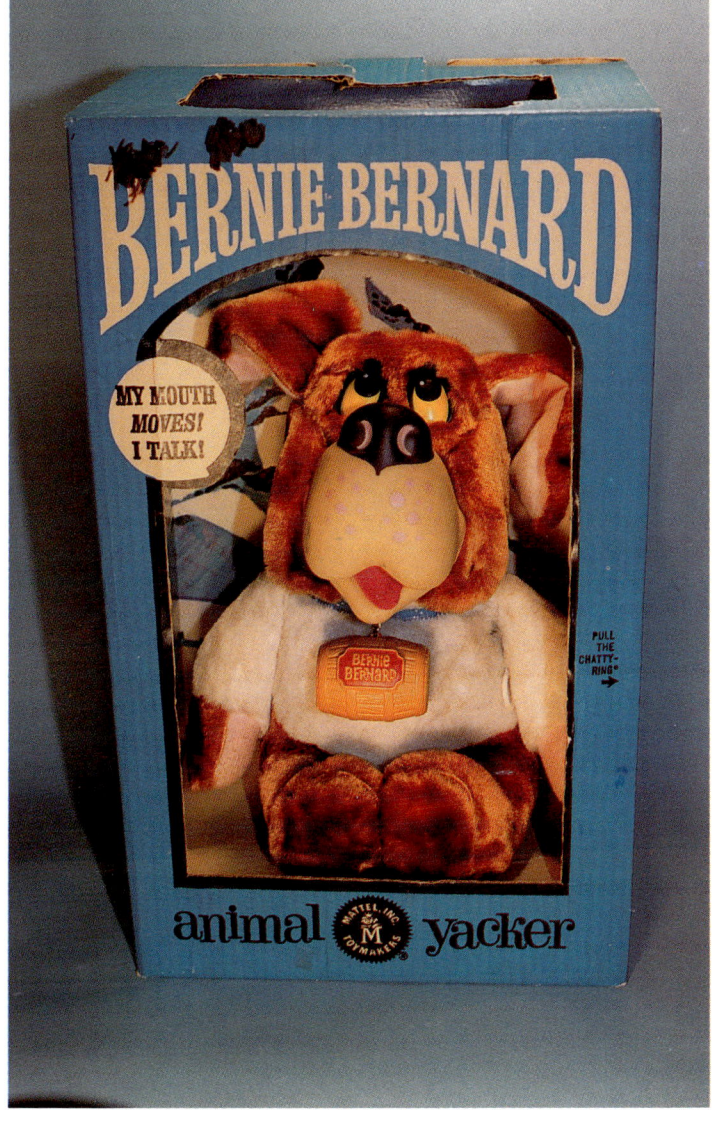

Bernie Bernard #5384 was 13" tall and another addition to the Animal Yacker line. This cuddly St. Bernard yodels as he talks! He is hard to find with his little blue collar and keg. $175-200. *Courtesy Michael Izzo Collection. Photo by Cris Johnson.*

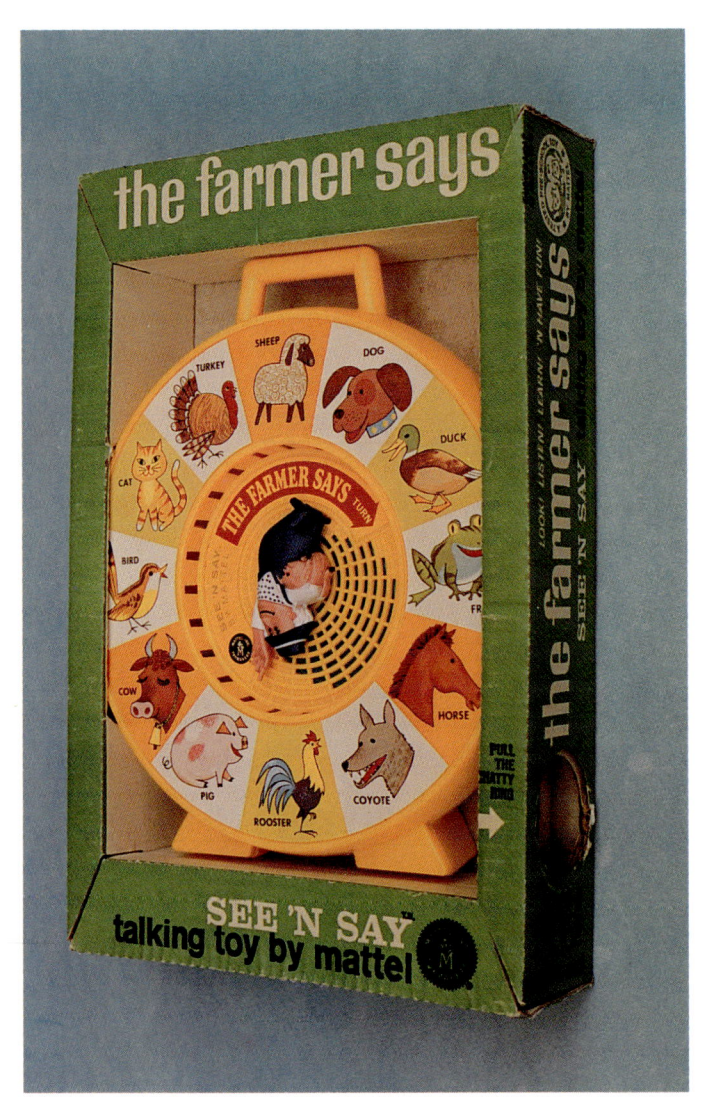

Spanning the years 1965-1966 Mattel issued a toy that has continued to the present. "See 'n Say" was a talking toy where the child could choose the phrase he or she wanted to hear. Used basically as a learning tool, the "See 'n Say" helped children learn ABC's or farm animal sounds. This one is called "Farmer Says." The child could turn the "pointer" and pull the string. $100-125. *Courtesy Michael Izzo Collection. Photo by Cris Johnson.*

The "Bee Says" See 'n Say was a fun way for children to learn the ABC's. The child would point the "Bee" to the desired letter and pull the string. One phrase might be, " 'B' is for Boy". $100-125. *Courtesy Michael Izzo Collection. Photo by Cris Johnson.*

J.C. Penney's Christmas catalogue from the early 1970s shows other talking See 'n Says. *Courtesy Cris Johnson Collection. Photo by Cris Johnson.*

Popeye #5366 was a Sears exclusive. This puppet later became available through S&H Green Stamps. He said eleven phrases in his cartoon voice. He is a rarity ... notice the thin vinyl arms. (he is missing his pipe.) $150-175.

Chapter 8 - 1967

The Barbie doll got her greatest makeover in 1967. Her face was entirely redesigned and she had a new longer hairstyle. Her twist 'n turn waist allowed her to be posed in many different positions.

The Liddle Kiddle dolls proved to be very popular and fast sellers, and some new additions were made to the existing line.

The talking dolls' popularity showed no sign of waning, and new dolls and toys continued to be designed and marketed. New for 1967 were:

    #3045 Baby's Hungry (non-talking)
    #3089 Baby Say 'n See
    #3049 Black Baby Say 'n See
    #3080 Baby Cheerful Tearful (non-talking)
    #3038 Talking Baby First Step
    #3047 Baby Walk 'n See (Sears exclusive, non-talking)
    #3044 Little Sister Look 'n Say (Sears exclusive)
    #5307 Mrs. Beasley
    #5334 Captain Kangaroo (Sears exclusive)
    #5395 Fuzby Bear
    #5396 Montana Mouse
    #5397 Lambie Pie
    #5306 King Kong and Bobby Bond
    #5386 Lilac and Sniffy Mint (Animal Yackers - two different dolls, one stock number)

Talking **Patter Pillows** were introduced in 1967; they were cotton "character" pillows with a voice unit inside:

    #5328 Puppy Patter
    #5326 Choo Choo Patter
    #5329 Tug Boat Patter
    #5330 Dolly Patter
    #5340 Bunny Patter

Talking Hand Puppets - 1967
    #5373 Monkees Puppet
    #5372 King Kong and Bobby Bond
    #5379 Bozo the Clown (Sears exclusive)
    #0376 Bugs Bunny
    #5380 Tom & Jerry

Baby Say 'n See #3089 was truly unique. When her string was pulled her mouth would move *and* her eyes would move side to side, as if she were looking around. She was 17" tall and said eleven different phrases. $150-200. *Courtesy Michael Izzo Collection. Photo by Cris Johnson.*

In 1967 a group of machine washable, poseable, plush, non-talking animals was issued. They were called **Flexi-Pets**:

   #5200 Monkey Shines (19" brown monkey)
   #5201 Leapin' Leopard (15" brown and white leopard)
   #5202 Sporty Spaniel (12" pink dog)
   #5203 Spunky Schnauzer (11" red dog)
   #5204 Houn' Dawg (16" yellow dog)
   #5205 Elegant Elephant (16" pink elephant)

Also out in 1967 were Googlies. These were plush, non-talking animals standing 14-15" tall; when their tummy was squeezed they would squeak and their eyes would spin round and round.

This black Baby Say 'n See #3049 said the same phrases as the white version. Mattel was beginning to produce more black dolls but this one from 1967 is still considered rare. $200-250. *Courtesy Michael Izzo Collection. Photo by Cris Johnson.*

The side view of Baby Say 'n See's box has some cute artwork that illustrates her features. *Courtesy Michael Izzo Collection. Photo by Cris Johnson.*

Talking Baby First Step #3038 was 18" tall and very popular in 1967. All the walking dolls by Mattel continued to be hot sellers—the talking feature was just one more reason to buy her. She had a new hairstyle and dress and said cute phrases like, "Let's walk to the park and go roller skating." Her talking mechanism was sealed inside her head. $100-125. *Courtesy Michael Izzo Collection. Photo by Cris Johnson.*

King Kong and Bobby Bond #5306, was 12" tall and inspired by the Saturday morning cartoon show of the same name. The little Bobby Bond character could be removed from King Kong's hand, but there was only one voice unit for both of them. When the string was pulled, one might hear Bobby Bond ask, "Where are we going now Kong?" and King Kong would answer in a thundering voice, "Home!" $250-300.

Captain Kangaroo #5334 was a Sears exclusive. He said eleven phrases in his T.V. voice provided by Bob Keeshan. He's 19" tall and his hat was removable. $100-125. *Courtesy Cris Johnson Collection. Photo by Cris Johnson.*

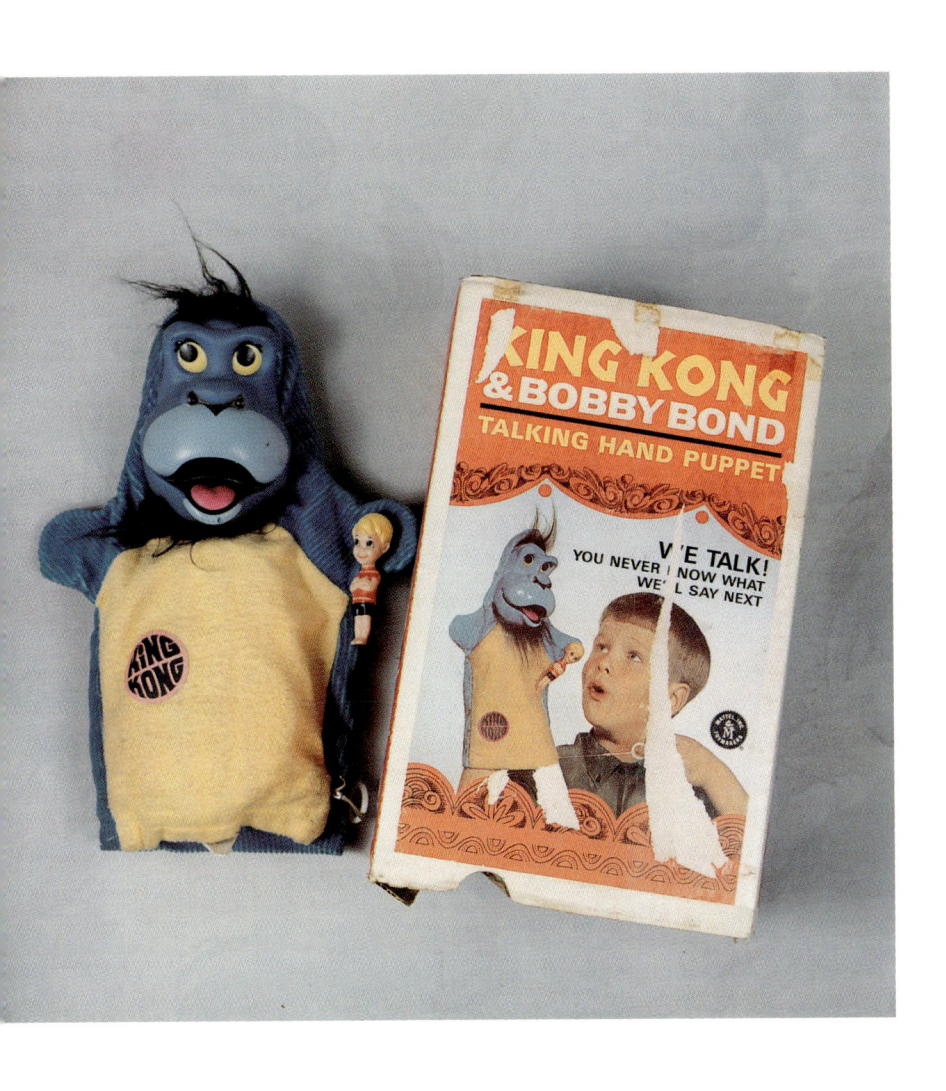

The talking puppet version of King Kong and Bobby Bond #5372 said the same phrases as the doll version, and Bobby could be removed too! $175-200. *Courtesy Graylen Becker Collection.*

Due to the popularity of the T.V. show *Family Affair* and the Mrs. Beasley doll (shown on page 88), many paper products became available. Whitman paper issued Mrs. Beasley and *Family Affair* paper dolls, puzzles, and books. $35-50. *Courtesy Cris Johnson Collection. Photo by Cris Johnson.*

Mrs. Beasley #5307 was a Mattel doll featured on the T.V. show *Family Affair*. She was 22" tall and said eleven phrases in a cute "granny" voice. $250-300. *Courtesy Cris Johnson Collection. Photo by Cris Johnson.*

Mrs. Beasley was 22" tall, and her skirt and collar were removable. She was the second doll that Mattel made wearing glasses. The first one was Charmin' Chatty in 1963.

88

Lilac and Sniffy Mint #5386, were new Animal Yackers for 1967. Both had the same stock number. Sniffy Mint was red and male, while Lilac was lavender and female. Each was sold separately and their mouths moved when they talked. Rare. *Photo by Cris Johnson.*

Here are Lilac and Sniffy Mint #5386, the talking skunks. Their mouths moved when their strings were pulled. Each said eleven phrases. Lilac's version of the Mattel slogan was, "You can tell by the smell, I'm swell!" Rare.

Sniffy Mint originally had a piece of peppermint candy attached to his ear. He also smells like peppermint, just as Lilac smells like lilac flowers. Rare. *Photo by Cris Johnson.*

Bunny Patter #5340 was a "Patter Pillow." This was a new idea, printed material sewn as a pillow with a voice unit inside. Patter Pillows were soft and cuddly and very popular; many were produced in different designs that were distinctively Mattel. $50-75.

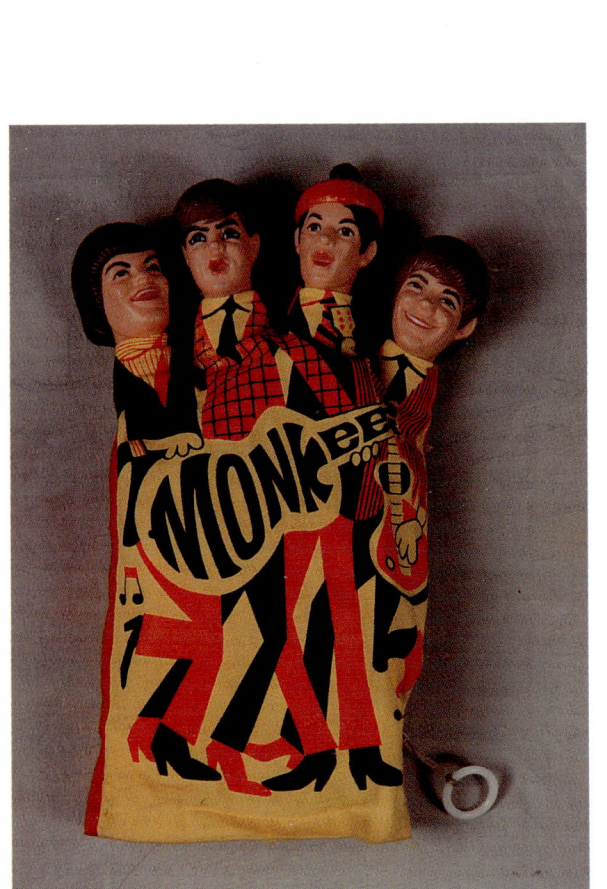

Here's a fun ad from the Sears Christmas Wish Book. It shows Captain Kangaroo #5334 and Bozo the Clown #0314, who was now a Sears exclusive too! *Courtesy Cris Johnson Collection. Photo by Cris Johnson.*

This Monkees puppet #5373 was called a finger puppet, because a finger was to be inserted inside each character. It was modeled after the cartoon show *The Monkees*, and when the string was pulled the voices were the real voices of Davy, Michael, Peter, and Micky. $150-200.

Chapter 9 - 1968

Mattel labored for years to perfect a talking voice unit that could fit inside the Barbie doll. In 1968, their efforts finally came to fruition - now Barbie could talk! The talking voice unit created for the Barbie doll also made it possible for smaller than usual talking dolls and toys to be designed.

The talking Barbie was hugely popular. Coupled with the success of the Liddle Kiddle doll line and newly issued talking dolls and toys, 1968 was one of Mattel's biggest years. The new dolls were:

- #3028 Baby Whisper
- #3023 Tippee Toes (non-talking, battery operated)
- #3020 Randi Reader (battery operated)
- #3039 Baby Smile 'n Frown (non-talking)
- #3025 Talking Baby 1st Step (new doll)
- #3024 Baby 1st Step (new doll, non-talking)
- #3010 Baby Small Talk
- #3011 Sister Small Talk
- #3027 Baby Small Walk (battery operated, non-talking)
- #3022 Black Talking Drowsy
- #8320 Spanish Speaking Drowsy
- #5349 Dr. Dolittle
- #5225 Talking Pushmi-Pullyu
- #5226 Talking Gentle Ben
- #5392 Lancelot Lion
- #5393 Tim Tim Tiger
- #5394 Rascal Rabbit

Talking Patter Pillows - 1968
- #5351 Mickey Mouse
- #5352 Donald Duck
- #5353 Off to see the Wizard
- #5350 Pink Pussycat
- #5346 Nite-Nite

Talking Hand Puppets - 1968
- #5364 Off to See the Wizard
- #5365 Dr. Dolittle
- #5366 Popeye (former Sears exclusive, now in regular line)

Talking Barbie #1115 was an item Mattel had worked on for years. Now their most famous doll could talk when her string was pulled. Her talking voice unit was used for other small dolls like Baby Small Talk #3010. $300 and up.

This ad was featured in a *LIFE* Magazine of the time. The three dolls in the top portion of the page are talkers: Barbie #1115 and Ken #1111, of course, and Julia the Nurse #1128, from the then popular T.V. show. The bottom half of the page shows Mattel's Tog'l Toys, snap together blocks. *Photo by Cris Johnson.*

Baby First Step #3024 was entirely overhauled in 1968. A new face mold, hairstyle, and hair color were used. She was 19" tall and got a new dress too. $50-75.

Baby Small Talk #3010 was only 10.75" tall and she said eight different phrases. Her voice unit was the same size as Talking Barbie's but she talked in an infant-like voice. $75-100.

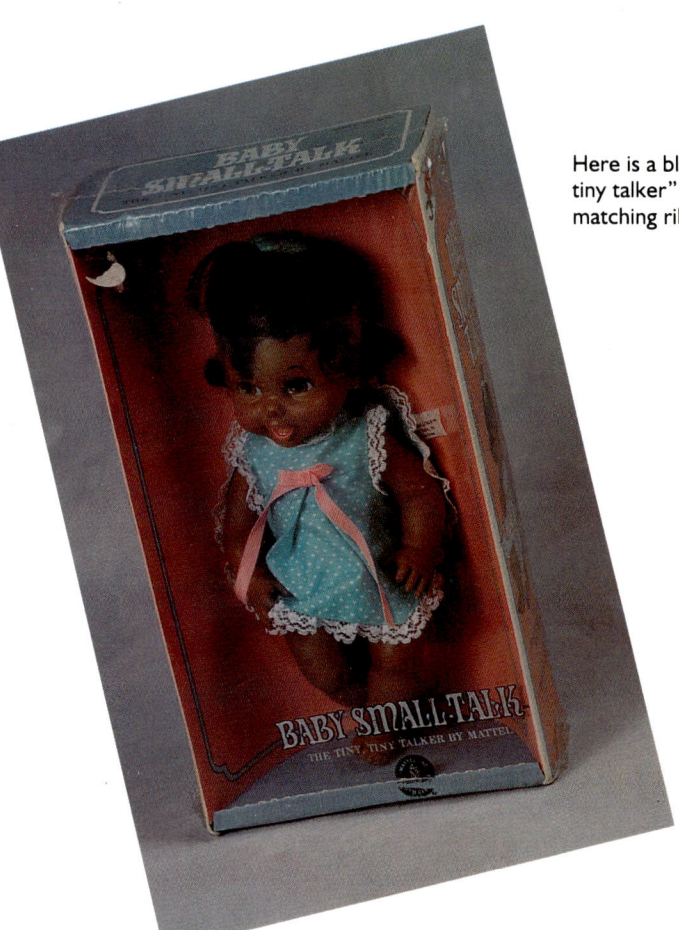

Here is a black Baby Small Talk in her original packaging. This "tiny, tiny talker" had a cute turquoise romper and panties, with a matching ribbon in her hair. She had no shoes. $100-150.

Extra clothes were available for the Small Talk dolls. Each came packaged in frame trays like Barbie doll clothes. Many of these clothes were tagged with the dolls' names. $25-40. *Courtesy Carmen Tickle/Cris Johnson Collections. Photo by Cris Johnson.*

Sister Small Talk #3011 was 13.75" tall and said eight groovy phrases. She had a cute mini dress and go-go boots. $75-100.

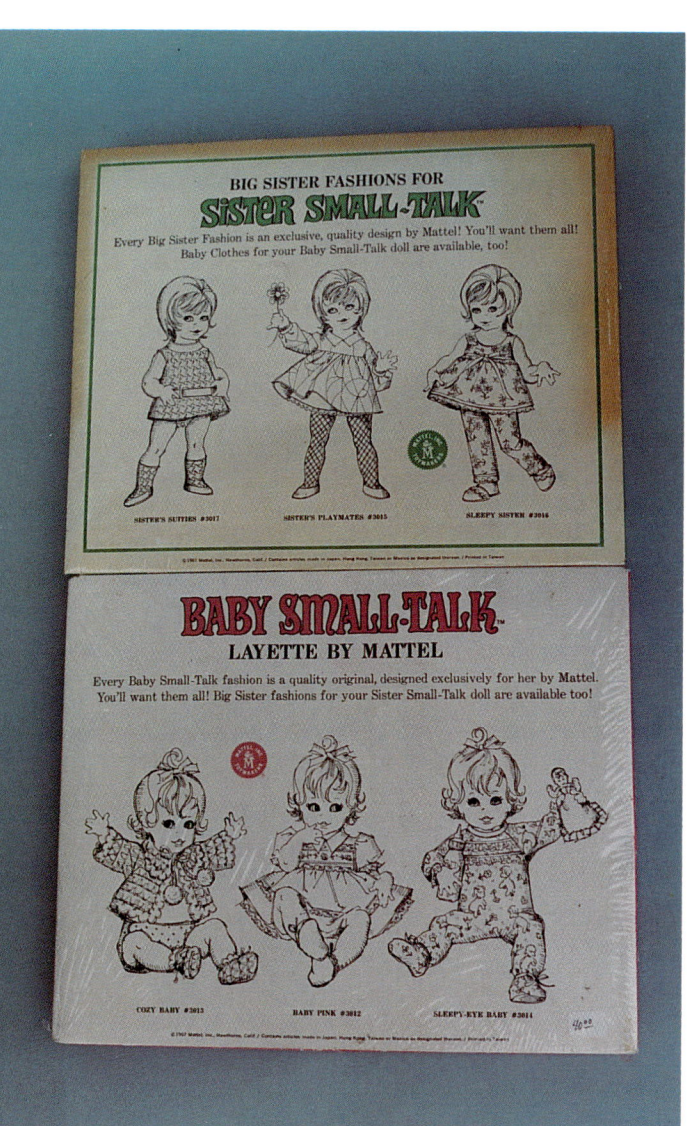

These are the illustrations on the back of the Small Talk clothes packages. They give a good idea of the other outfits that were sold separately. *Courtesy Carmen Tickle/Cris Johnson Collections. Photo by Cris Johnson.*

Baby Small Walk #3027 was a 10.75" version of Baby First Step. She was battery operated and walked with or without her toys. The doll was also sold individually. $75-100. *Courtesy Cris Johnson Collection. Photo by Cris Johnson.*

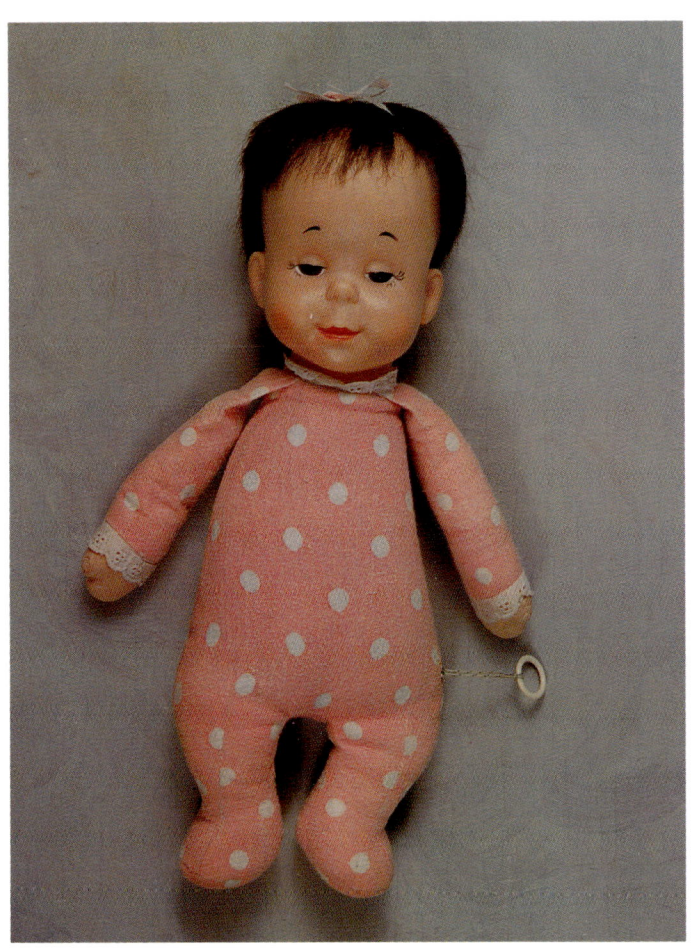

Drowsy got a different look in 1968 with new pajamas. The "kitty" PJ's were replaced by pink flannel ones with white dots. All Drowsy's had blonde hair until 1968. This one speaks Spanish and she also has painted brown eyes. A black Drowsy was issued too, but if you find one with light skin and brown hair ... she speaks Spanish! This one is from the mid 1970s; it was then that the vinyl hands were replaced with cloth mitten ones. $75-100.

Dr. Dolittle #5349 was based on the title character of the movie with the same name. He stood 24" tall and said eleven different phrases in his movie voice, provided by Rex Harrison. $125-150.

Talking Pushmi-Pullyu #5225 was a character in the movie *Dr. Dolittle*. It was as unusual a toy as it was a movie character, but kids everywhere loved it. It said eleven different phrases. $125-150.

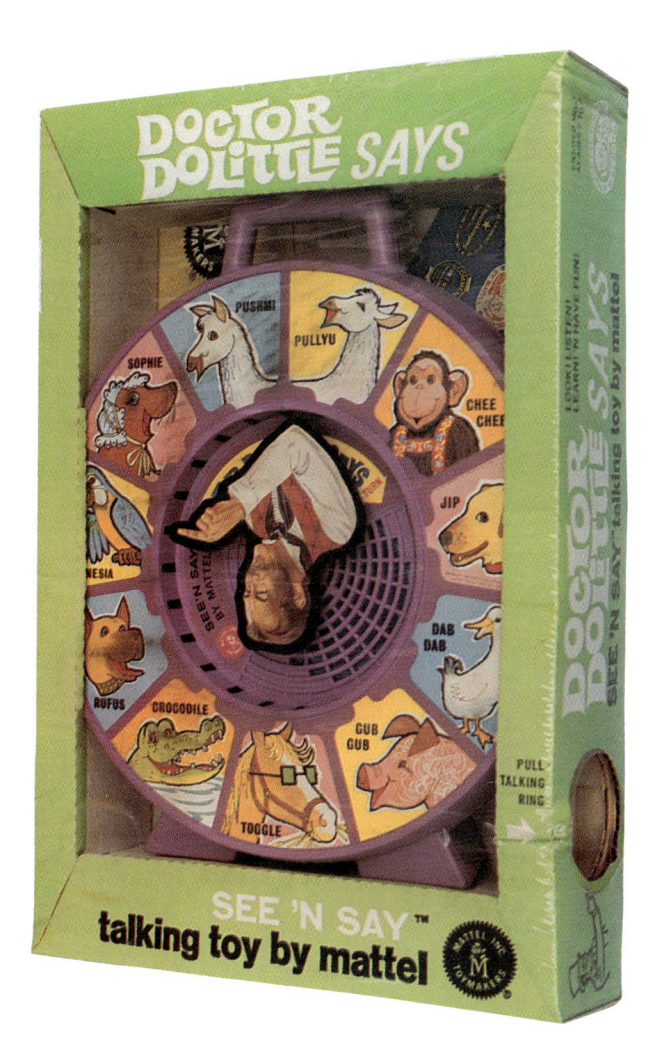

A talking See 'n Say toy was devoted entirely to Dr. Dolittle. He was the Doctor who could talk to the animals, so all the talking movie animals were featured too. $100-125. *Courtesy Michael Izzo Collection. Photo by Cris Johnson.*

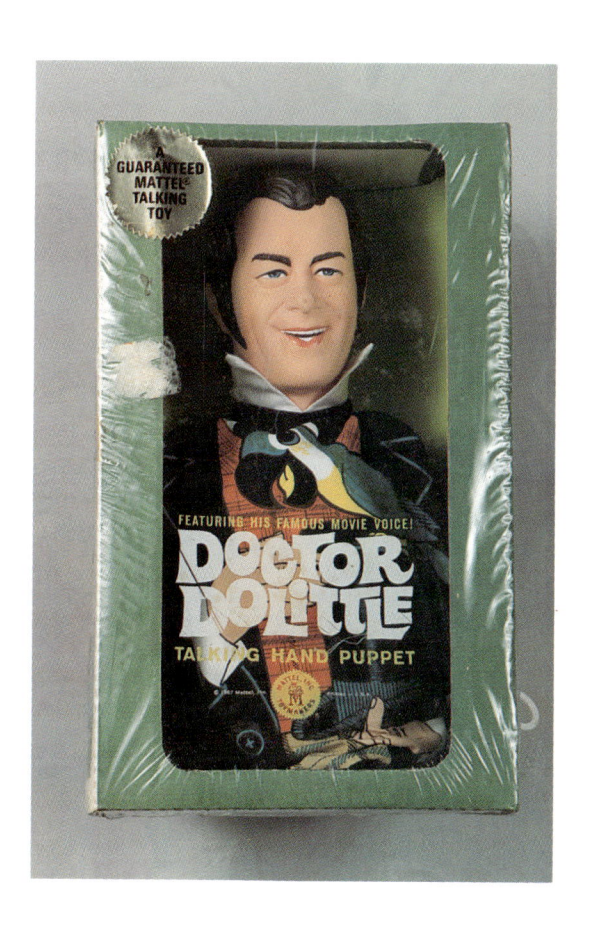

Off to See the Wizard puppet #5364, was made in the same style as the Monkees puppet #5373. A finger could be put inside each character, and the puppet said eleven different phrases. This was based on the T.V. cartoon show, so the characters do not resemble the MGM movie characters. $150-200. *Courtesy Cris Johnson Collection. Photo by Cris Johnson.*

Here is the Dr. Dolittle talking hand puppet #5365. This had the same voice unit as the doll and says the same eleven phrases. $150-200.

97

Here is the back of the Off to See the Wizard box; you can see the T.V. cartoon characters in the background. Both the show and puppet were very popular. *Courtesy Cris Johnson Collection. Photo by Cris Johnson.*

This back view of Nite-Nite #5346 "Patter Pillow" shows the cute attention to detail that made these dolls so much fun.

Nite-Nite #5346 was a new "Patter Pillow" for 1968. Also issued in 1968 were Patter Pillows of Mickey Mouse, Donald Duck, and Off to See the Wizard. $50-75.

Chapter 10 - 1969

Mattel was still the number one toy maker in the world, but the effect of cutbacks was now starting to show in the production lines. Dolls were no longer available in different hair colors, and painted eyes replaced the "go-to-sleep" version. With very few exceptions, none of the talking dolls had an extra wardrobe available separately. Often plastic bags with the doll's name printed on them were used as packaging instead of boxes.

In 1969 more and more dolls were issued in series, such as Storybook Dolls, Cuddles Snuggles, etc. The new dolls issued were:

    #3061 Dancerina (non-talking)
    #3063 Swingy (non-talking)
    #3117 Black Swingy (non-talking)
    #3051 Baby Fun (non-talking)
    #3106 Bouncy Baby (non-talking)
    #3118 Black Bouncy Baby (non-talking)
    #3107 Buffy and Mrs. Beasley
    #3116 Baby Sing-a-Song (Sears exclusive)
    #8360 Spanish Speaking Baby Small Talk
    #5235 Mr. Potts
    #5215 Buzzy Bear

Storybook Dolls
    #3065 Cinderella
    #3066 Little Bo Peep
    #3067 Goldilocks

Roarin' Twenties Ragdolls
    #5213 Flo
    #5214 Flossie

Cuddles Snuggles
    #5232 Pink Nibbles the Mouse
    #5231 White Lovey the Lamb
    #5230 Orange Biffy the Bear

Patter Pillows - 1969
    #5266 Goofy Patter
    #5250 Brown Bear
    #5251 Circus Clown
    #5265 Tinker Bell
    #4204 Puppy Patter (S&H Green Stamps exclusive)

Talking Hand Puppets
    #5211 Larry the Lion
    #5212 Maurice Monkey
    #5210 Bernardo St. Bernard
    #4205 Popeye (S&H Greenstamps exclusive)

Dancerina #3061 was an instant success in 1969. This ballerina doll was akin to Baby First Step in that she walked, except that Dancerina walked on her toes. The doll was operated by the knob in the center of her crown, and with a flip of the switch she could toe dance and pirouette. An instruction folder and cardboard record of Tchaikovsky was included. Note that this doll cannot stand on her own. $85-100.

This is the instruction folder included with the Dancerina doll. As you can see, this doll could pose in many different positions. She was a large doll at 24" tall.

This Dancerina ad was featured in *LIFE* Magazine in 1969. It really captured the essence of little girls' dreams. Dancerina was another great success for Mattel. *Photo by Cris Johnson.*

Swingy #3063 was another doll similar to Baby First Step. The idea here was that she "danced" instead of walked. She was 20" tall, her head moved back and forth, and she would swing her arms. Like Dancerina, Swingy came with a cardboard record of dance music. Instead of "The Nutcracker" though, the music was Big Band Swing! $85-100.

This is Swingy's instruction and registration card. Cards similar to this were included with all Mattel dolls.

101

Mr. Potts #5235 was one of the main characters in the children's movie, *Chitty Chitty Bang Bang*. Mattel had all rights for merchandising the characters from the movie. Mr. Potts was a rag style doll completely stuffed, his face a caricature of Dick Van Dyke, who played the part in the movie. Dick Van Dyke also provided this doll's voice. "Truly Scrumptious" was another movie character transformed into a talking doll, only she was Barbie doll sized. Other dolls of the cast were produced in Liddle Kiddle size—about 2" tall or less. $125-150.

Little Bo Peep was another "Storybook doll" styled from the Sister Small Talk doll's mold. She said eight different phrases. *Courtesy Cris Johnson Collection. Photo by Cris Johnson.* $75-100.

Cinderella #3065 was a "Storybook doll" styled from the Sister Small Talk doll's mold. Sold separately were Little Bo Peep and Goldilocks. They were delightful dolls and very popular, each said eight phrases and came with her own storybook. $75-100.

Buffy and Mrs. Beasley #3107 was another talking doll modeled on characters from the popular T.V. show, *Family Affair*. Buffy was the niece on the show and she owned a doll called Mrs. Beasley. This doll was also made from the Sister Small Talk doll mold, just like the "Storybook" series. She said eight phrases. $200-250. *Courtesy Cris Johnson Collection. Photo by Cris Johnson.*

Flossie #5214 was one of a pair of "Roarin' Twenties Ragdolls." The other one was called Flo #5213, and her dress was a different color. Both were 11.5" tall. Note that the "jewel necklace" is hard to find. $50-75. *Courtesy Cris Johnson Collection. Photo by Cris Johnson.*

Liddle Kiddles Talking Townhouse #5154, was a play house for the Mattel line of dolls called "Liddle Kiddles." Two of the dolls are illustrated on the side of the vinyl house. The scale of these dolls, approximately 2", was quite small, especially when compared with Chatty Cathy's 20" and Barbie's 11.5". When the string was pulled on the side of the house, eleven phrases were heard in a different "Kiddles" voice. There is a small elevator inside and one phrase is, "Elevator going up!" $75-100.

Maurice Monkey #5212, was one of the new larger style of talking hand puppets. The face mold was once Chester O'Chimp from 1965. This version speaks with a French accent when his string is pulled. Puppets were also issued with the face molds of Larry the Lion and Bernie Bernard. $150-175. *Photo by Sharon Harrington.*

Mattel-O-Phone was a toy originally issued in 1965. Small records could be changed in a slot located on one side of the telephone, and when a button was pushed one could hear different phrases from different toy characters. One record featured Barbie and Skipper. The 1965 phone was red, but in 1969 Mattel devoted an entire pink Mattel-O-Phone to Barbie and her friends! $200-250. *Courtesy Cris Johnson Collection. Photo by Cris Johnson.*

Chapter 11 - 1970

A decade had passed since the original Chatty Cathy was introduced and five years since she was discontinued. In 1970, Mattel decided to re-issue new Chatty dolls. Included were Chatty Cathy, Chatty Baby, and Tiny Chatty Baby. These dolls bore no resemblance to the earlier ones, and they said completely different phrases. The voice for the re-issued Chatty Cathy was provided by Maureen McCormick, who played Marsha on *The Brady Bunch*. No extra wardrobes were available separately.

The body mold used for the new Chatty Cathy was the same one that had been used for Singin' Chatty. The mold mark was altered and looked like this:

```
©1964 MATTEL, INC.
HAWTHORNE, CALIF. USA
PATENTED IN USA
PATENTED IN CANADA 1962
OTHER PATENTS PENDING
```

This mold and mold mark were used for several talking dolls afterward. Since this mark still reads "1964," the collector must look at the nape of the doll's neck, just below the hairline, for the imprint showing the actual date of the doll's issue.

Some new doll series were also initiated in 1970, called Pretty Pairs and Wet Noodles. These were small, non-talking, fun dolls. The Pretty Pairs were 5" poseable dolls that had tiny dolls of their own, and Wet Noodles were 5" longhaired dolls that came with two ounces of shampoo.

Also introduced were Patter Pals; these were simply Patter Pillows with arms and legs.

New for 1970:
#3130 Chatty Cathy (re-issued)
#3131 Chatty Baby (re-issued)
#3057 Tiny Chatty Baby (re-issued)
#3141 Black Chatty Cathy (re-issued)
#3143 Baby Go Bye-Bye (non-talking)
#3147 Black Baby Go Bye-Bye (non-talking)
#3134 Sketchy (non-talking)
#3122 Baby Walk 'n Play (non-talking)
#3123 Baby Dancerina (non-talking)
#3135 Tiny Swingy (non-talking)
#3132 Snow White (addition to Story Book line)
#5220 Great Big Beautiful Bertha
#5221 Somersalty (a turnover doll)
#3149 Baby Flip Flop (a turnover doll, J.C. Penney exclusive)
#5233 Grandma Doll (Sears exclusive)
#5218 Puff the Dog (from television's *To Rome with Love*)
#5303 Curli Pup (Sears exclusive)
#5219 Barry Bear
#5223 Cat in the Hat

Patter Pals - 1970
#5256 Pep Talk
#5254 Happy Talk
#5255 Beddie Bye Talk

Patter Pillow - 1970
#5267 Red Riding Hood and Wolf (a turnover doll)

Talking Hand Puppet - 1970
#5217 Myrtle (from television's *My Three Sons*)

Pretty Pairs - Non-talking
#1133 Lori 'n Rori
#1135 Angie n' Tangie
#1134 Nan 'n Fran
#3566 Buffy and Mrs. Beasley

Wet Noodles
#3850 Fuschia, Lime Green and Orange (color variations)

Here is the new Tiny Chatty Baby sitting between two Baby Small Talk dolls from 1968. One can see instantly that they were made from the same molds.

Chatty Cathy #3130, was a re-issue Chatty doll. The only thing that brought to mind the original Chatty Cathy in this doll were the freckles. These new dolls were comparatively inexpensive to produce. The eyes were painted and the hair was blond ... no more choices of eye and hair color. She said eleven phrases in a new voice provided by Maureen McCormick of *The Brady Bunch* fame. $75-100. *Courtesy Cyndie Steffen Collection. Photo by Cris Johnson.*

Tiny Chatty Baby #3057 was actually a Baby Small Talk doll with brown eyes and fluffy blond hair. This new 10.75" version of Tiny Chatty Baby was completely different from the original. An updated version of Chatty Baby, #3131, was also issued. $75-100.

Snow White #3132 was a new addition to the "Storybook" small talk dolls. She was very popular, as were all the dolls in the Storybook line. Each came with her own storybook. $75-100.

Great Big Beautiful Bertha #5220, was a "dancing" doll. Her feet could be strapped to a child's feet so the child could dance with her. She stood almost 4' tall and said eleven different phrases. $100-125. Courtesy Michael Izzo Collection. Photo by Michael Izzo.

Baby Flip-Flop #3149 was a J.C. Penney exclusive. She, like Somersalty, could stand on her flat head. Also a turnover talker, her different phrases were said five upside down and five rightside up. $100-150.

Somersalty #5221 can say four phrases while standing upright and four different phrases standing on his flat head. He was called a "turnover talker!" $100-150. Courtesy Michael Izzo Collection. Photo by Cris Johnson.

Grandma #5233, was a Sears exclusive designed by Joyce Miller. This little granny said ten different phrases. She proved so popular that the Grandpa doll followed a year later. $100-125.

Curli Pup #5303, was a Sears exclusive. This little poodle also came with curlers and a hairbrush. $75-100.

Cat in the Hat #5223 was a 23" talking Dr. Suess character. This was the first Dr. Suess doll made by Mattel. Many would follow! $350 and up. *Courtesy Cris Johnson Collection. Photo by Cris Johnson.*

Pep Talk #5256 was a new kind of Patter Pillow. These dolls had arms and were called Patter Pals. This little ball player said eleven different phrases like, "Let's hear some chattah ... eh battah battah battah." $50-75.

Happy Talk #5254, was a Patter Pal that said eleven happy phrases. She is cut from the same pattern as both Pep Talk and another Patter Pal, #5255 Beddie Bye Talk. $50-75.

Myrtle #5217 was a featured talking toy on the T.V. show *My Three Sons*. She was the "pal" to Dodie, a character on the show. This was very much like Buffy's relationship to Mrs. Beasley on T.V.'s *Family Affair*. $175-200.

Talking Service Center was used with a line of toy cars called "Hot Wheels." It was made of vinyl and similar to the Liddle Kiddle house. It said ten different things. $75-100. *Courtesy Michael Izzo Collection. Photo by Cris Johnson.*

111

Talking Command Console was another talker aimed at boys. Nine phrases were said at random when the string was pulled. This was from the mid 1970s and featured "Major Matt Mason," a Mattel action figure. $150-175. *Courtesy Michael Izzo Collection. Photo by Cris Johnson.*

This is the Talking Command Console, vinyl and very durable. It said nine phrases when the string was pulled. This is a toy to be used with "Major Matt Mason," the Mattel action figure. *Courtesy Michael Izzo Collection. Photo by Cris Johnson.*

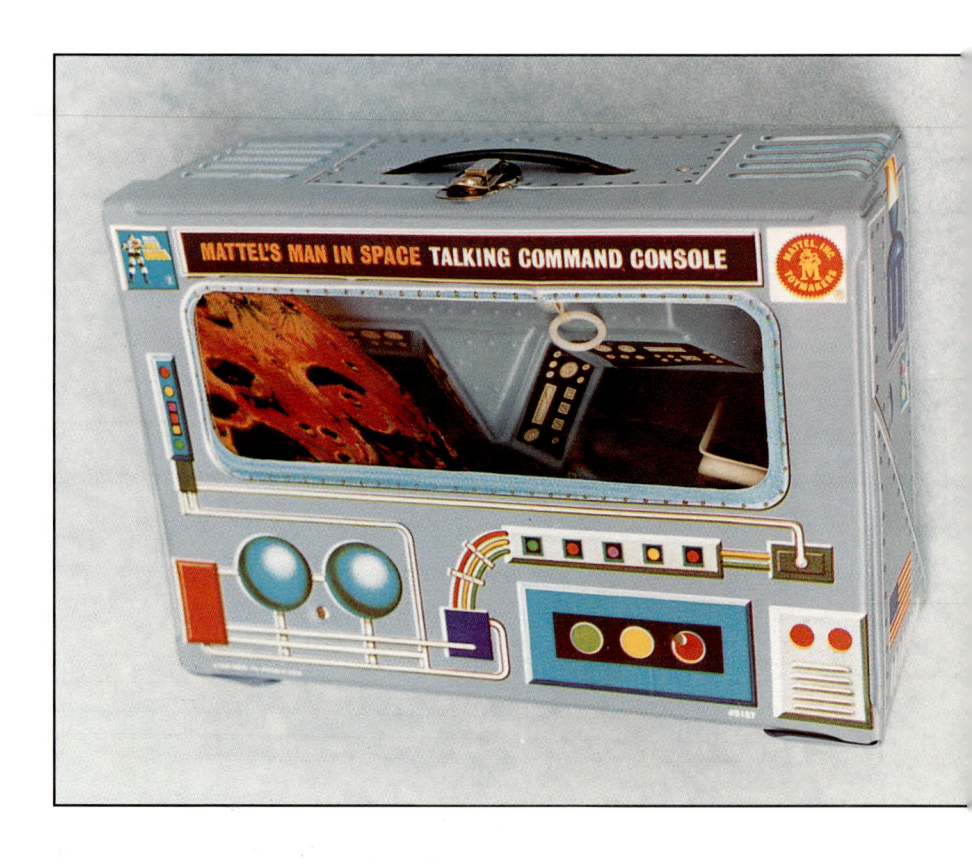

Talking Storybooks became available during this period. They used the "See 'n Say" concept. The dial could be turned to a certain mark and when the string was pulled, the toy would say a certain phrase. Inside the Storybooks, children could read along! $100-125.

Here is the inside of a Talking Storybook. A child only needed to open the book, turn the dial, line up the pointers, and pull the string. The voice unit would then say the appropriate phrase. Each story was about eighteen pages long, mounted on a cardboard box that contained the voice unit. $100-125.

Chapter 12 - 1971

By 1971, Mattel was experiencing some major corporate and financial troubles. These problems seemed impossible after a decade of manufacturing the world's most popular dolls and toys, yet cutbacks and money-saving measures had been going on for a few years. A gallant effort was still made to issue wonderful playthings, but sometimes the efforts fell short. In this author's opinion, quality was compromised, frills and extras were stopped.

Live Action and Malibu Barbies came out in 1971, and the Liddle Kiddle doll line that had debuted in 1966 ended.

Other dolls issued in 1971 were:
- #3160 Shoppin' Sheryl (non-talking)
- #3171 Busy Becky (non-talking)
- #3151 Timey Tell
- #3159 Talking Baby Tender Love
- #3163 Living Baby Tender Love (non-talking)
- #3166 Baby Lovelight (non-talking)
- #3164 Valerie (non-talking)
- #3167 Black Valerie (non-talking)
- #5224 Mother Goose
- #3169 Talking Twosome (Sears exclusive)
- #5355 Paula Bear
- #5259 Humpty Dumpty (turnover talker)
- #5277 Bozo Patter Pal

Baby Beans (12" Bean Bag dolls)
- #5244 Bedsie Beans (yawning)
- #5245 Booful Beans (grinning)
- #5246 Bitty Beans (smiling)

Small Shots (15" dolls that skate on Hot Wheels track)
- #3887 Daffy Taffy and Dizzy Lizzy
- #3880 Red Hot Red and Sillie Millie
- #3877 Nifty Nan!
- #3876 Breezy Bridget!
- #3875 Daredevil Dexter!

Talk-a-littles (6-7" Rag Characters)
- #5241 Toofums
- #5243 Roscoe
- #5257 Sassie

Talking Dr. Suess Characters
- #5262 Cat in the Hat
- #5261 Hedwig Bird
- #5239 Horton the Elephant
- #5263 Yertle the Turtle
- #5248 Cat in the Hat puppet

Timey Tell #3151, was a talker that told time! One could move the hands on her wristwatch and she would tell the time and the appropriate activity. She stood 17.5" tall and when her string was pulled she might say, "It's four o'clock, let's have a tea party." It was a fun way to learn to tell time. $75-100. *Courtesy Cris Johnson Collection. Photo by Cris Johnson.*

Timey Tell is shown here in the black version. She is made from the same mold and says the same phrases. She also came with all the same accouterments. $75-100.

Timey Tell came with many different props for her suggested activities. Included were things to have tea, brush one's teeth, have lunch, or read a story.

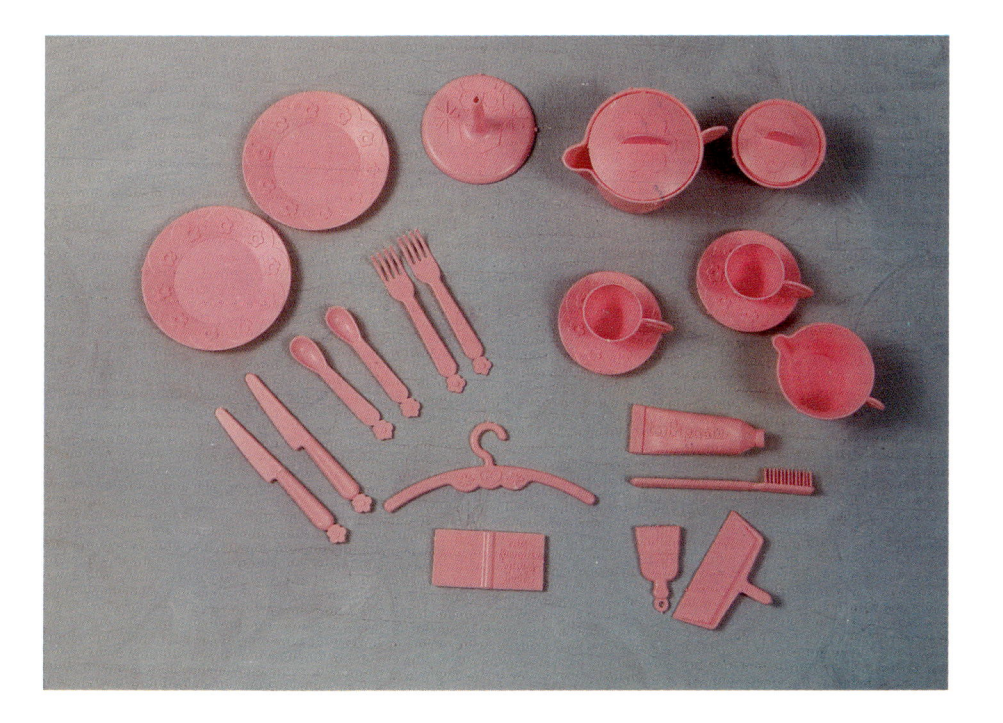

115

Mother Goose #5224 was an adorable talking doll. She was 20" tall while sitting, but seemed a little bulky because of her large plastisol head and hat. She said ten phrases from Nursery Rhymes. $75-100.

This fun ad is from the Sear's Wish Book. It shows several Mattel talking dolls, like the Talking Twosome #3169, a Sears exclusive. These two dolls both talk—the 16" baby says ten phrases and her little dolly says eight phrases. Also, you can see the Talking Baby doll Pajama Bag which was a Sears exclusive too. Notice the Bozo the Clown Patter Pal #5277, he's a hard-to-find Sears exclusive. *Courtesy Cris Johnson Collection. Photo by Cris Johnson.*

116

Toofums #5241, was a 6" rag doll that was part of a trio called "Talk-a-Littles." Each was sold separately and said eight phrases. This one is missing her little romper but is cute just the same. $50-75. *Photo by Cris Johnson.*

This doll is called a Talking Twin, because she has a sister dressed in the same outfit, only yellow! Her sister also has blonde hair. They have the same face mold as Baby Small Walk. Each says eight fun phrases. They were sold separately. $75-100 each.

This is the back side of Toofums #5241. Her missing romper matched the back of her bonnet. The tag identifies her as a Talk-a-Little. *Photo by Cris Johnson.*

Cat in the Hat #5262 is shown here in his 11" version. These were eventually called Small Talkers; also included were Horton the Elephant and Yertle the Turtle. Each was sold separately. $150-200.

Hedwig Bird #5261 was an addition to the Dr. Suess talking toy line. It was 11" tall in its sitting position. Hedwig said eight different phrases. $225-250. *Courtesy Michael Izzo Collection. Photo by Michael Izzo.*

Chatter Buggies were talking cars for little boys and girls. They were part pull toy and part talker. Each said eight phrases. $50-75. *Courtesy Michael Izzo Collection. Photo by Cris Johnson.*

This Jack in the Box was unusual because he also talked when the string was pulled. Called the Talking Jack in the Box, he was actually a "clown in the box" and was issued in 1971. He came with a wagon. $75-100. *Courtesy Michael Izzo Collection. Photo by Cris Johnson.*

Flip Wilson and Geraldine was a flip over doll that said ten different phrases. Based on Flip Wilson's comedy show, the doll says five phrases as Flip and five as his character Geraldine, Flip Wilson provided the voices! $40-60.

Tamu was put out by Mattel through the company Shindana and Operation Bootstrap. She said eleven phrases like, "I'm proud mama, like you." $100-125.

Boomy Boomer, the drum, and Plinky Plunker, the piano, were talking instruments. Each said eleven phrases complete with sound effects. $50-75.

Smartipig was a See n' Say talking bank. He would count the money and tell how much you had saved. He said seven phrases, all about money. $75-100. *Courtesy Michael Izzo Collection. Photo by Cris Johnson.*

Here's another scene from the J.C. Penney Christmas Catalogue. This shows the Talking Time Clock, one more fun toy to help children learn to tell time! *Courtesy Cris Johnson Collection. Photo by Cris Johnson.*

Here's an ad from the J.C. Penney Christmas catalogue. It shows Smartipig and some other toys. It's always fun to see these toys with their original prices! *Courtesy Cris Johnson Collection. Photo by Cris Johnson.*

121

Chapter 13 - 1972

Despite problems in the company, Mattel continued to manufacture some amusing, if not interesting dolls. There were dolls like Hi Dottie, a battery operated talker that came with two telephones. The child could squeeze either the telephone receiver or the doll's arm to activate the doll and make it talk. Best Friend Cynthia was a 19" doll that had changeable records, calling forth memories of Charmin' Chatty from nearly a decade ago. She spoke with a battery operated voice unit, and was started by pressing a button on her back. There were also Talk Ups, 4.5" inch dolls that talked when their heads were pulled up.

Here's everyone who was issued in 1972:
#3185 Hi Dottie
#3177 Baby Play-a-lot
#3187 Baby Kiss & Talk
#3186 Tearful Baby Tender Love (non-talking)
#3188 Tiny Baby Tender Love (non-talking)
#3172 Best Friend Cynthia
#5289 Cuddly Beans (non-talking)
#5282 Teachy Talk

Small Talkers (9-11" Rag Characters)
#5288 Bullwinkle
#5263 Yertle the Turtle
#5285 Bugs Bunny
#5262 Cat in the Hat

Small Shots
Each doll now has a vehicle instead of skates.

Talk Ups
#4022 Funny Talk (brown hair)
#4021 Silly Talk (blond hair)

Bean Pals
#5290 Bear Pal
#5291 Puppy Pal

Talking Party Liners (election year dolls with political talk)
#5294 Rag Elephant
#5293 Rag Donkey

Barbie was available at this time as "Walk Lively" and "Busy," among others. Busy Barbie used the same principal as Shoppin' Sheryl - one hand was magnetized and she could "hold" things.

This illustration is from the back of "best friend Cynthia" #3172 Mint-in-Package outfit. It shows the doll in three different outfits available separately. The actual doll stood 19" tall and resembled the 1980s Super Size Barbie doll. Cynthia could say many different phrases because her record could be changed. She and Charmin' Chatty were the only Mattel dolls to have changeable records. The records were smaller and had general titles like "Indoor activities" or "Outdoor activities." Cynthia was battery operated, and to make her talk one pushed a button in the center of her back. $100-125.

Here is the Mint-in-Package outfit for "best friend Cynthia." Notice the small record in the upper left hand corner. Each outfit had its own record. $25-40.

Cat in the Hat hand puppet was another extraordinary Dr. Suess toy by Mattel. It said ten different phrases in his cartoon voice. $200-225. *Courtesy Cris Johnson Collection. Photo by Cris Johnson.*

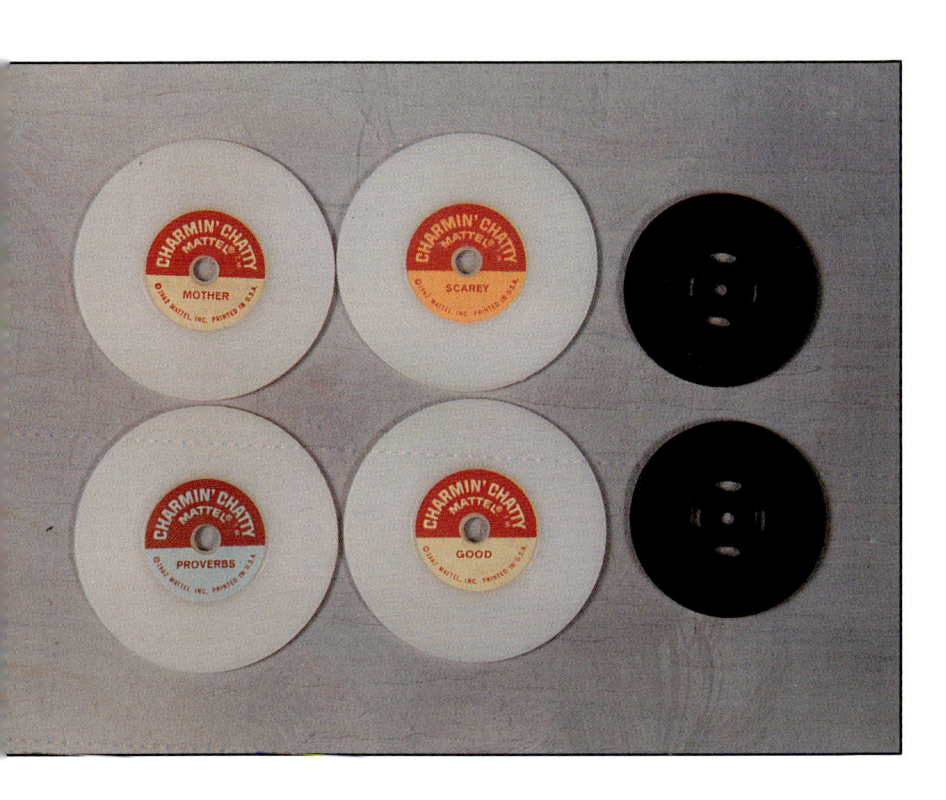

This picture shows the difference in size between Charmin' Chatty's records from 1963 (on the left) and best friend Cynthia's records from 1972 (on the right).

Teachy Talk #5282 said ten different phrases about good grooming. She gave kids instructions on lacing shoes, buttoning and zipping clothes. She also had a brush and comb. $50-75.

Bugs Bunny-Small Talker #5285 was 9" tall. He said eight different phrases. Bullwinkle was another of the Small Talkers. $100-125. *Courtesy Cris Johnson Collection. Photo by Cris Johnson.*

Talk Ups were 4.5" dolls that talked when their heads were pulled up. One was brown haired #4022 Funny Talk, who had the voice of actress Joanne Worley from T.V.'s *Laugh In*. The other, #4021 Silly Talk, had blonde hair. When their heads were pulled one phrase was, "I've lost my head over you!" $50-75.

Chapter 14 - 1973 and Beyond

By 1973, as the times changed, Mattel Inc. Toy makers seemed to be moving beyond the talking doll era. Many talkers were still on the market, but tended to be re-issues of earlier dolls. Talking Bugs Bunny, for example, had been in stores for ten years and continued to be available for many more years in one form or another.

The trend at this time was toward dolls with life-like skin, such as the Tender Love dolls. Bean bag dolls like Baby Beans were also very popular. A Talking Baby Beans was issued in 1973.

Peachy and Her Puppets was an interesting addition to the talking doll line. She could hold puppets in her hand and talk about each one when her string was pulled. Her secret? The stem on the bottom of each puppet was a different length. When one of the stems was put in the hole in her right hand, it would push down a button inside the hand. Peachy would then say the appropriate things.

Peachy would come back ten years later as Chatty Patty. Her hairstyle and other features would be different but she would be able to say the appropriate phrases for what she was holding.

A fun doll issued at this time was Saucy. She was 15" tall, and when her right arm was moved up and behind her head her facial expressions would change into ridiculous contortions. Sometimes her eyes would cross too. She was a non-talker.

A new idea called Quick Curl Hair was introduced in 1974, and a doll called Cathy Quick Curl became very popular. Tiny copper wires were enmeshed in her hair, so it could be wrapped around your finger in a curl and then stay that way. Barbie and her friends got Quick Curl hair too! It made their hair very styleable.

In 1977, Chatter Chums were introduced. They were 10" talking figures whose mouths opened and closed when they talked; actually the whole top of their heads moved when the string was pulled. A picture of the Bugs Bunny Chatter Chum is featured in Chapter 6. Other Chatter Chums were issued of Mickey Mouse and Pink Panther.

1983 was the year that Chatty Patty was issued. She was simply the same doll as Peachy and Her Puppets from 1973, but with a different hairstyle and outfit. It had been over twenty years since Chatty Cathy was first introduced and over ten since she had been re-issued.

Talking dolls were barely heard of anymore by the 1990s, when out of the blue Mattel issued a new talking Barbie. The talking voice unit in these dolls was powered by watch batteries instead of a pull string. Little girls needed to push a button to hear her talk. "Teen Talk Barbie" created an uproar when she was heard to say that she thought math was a hard subject at school. Women's groups were enraged because they thought their gender was being stereotyped. But never fear, women could of course do anything and Barbie had proven it. She had been a teenage fashion model, an astronaut, and a doctor among many other things.

The infamous Teen Talk Barbie was available for one year only, in 1992. She was followed by Super Talk Barbie in 1994, who said more than one thousand different things. Super Talk Barbie was available for only one year as well.

Perhaps the new talking Barbies will signal a re-emergence of Mattel's talking dolls and lead to a second heyday like the first one in the 1960s when Chatty Cathy was the star.

Peachy and her Puppets at 17" tall was an interesting talking doll. She could say three phrases in her own voice, while the other eight phrases were for her "puppets." Notice the hole in her right hand—the small stem at the base of each puppet was inserted in this hole. Each puppet had a different length stem, which pushed a button inside her hand down to different depths. In this way the doll could say two appropriate phrases for each puppet when her string was pulled. $75-100. *Courtesy Cris Johnson Collection. Photo by Cris Johnson.*

Mattel was called upon in the late 1960s and early 1970s to produce advertising dolls. These ranged from a Barbie doll dressed in nothing but a tin can (for a canning company), to talking dolls for other corporations. One of these dolls was "Charlie Tuna," made for the Star-Kist tuna company. A plastic bag was often used as packaging during these times of economic cutbacks. $100-150. *Courtesy Carmen Tickle Collection. Photo by Cris Johnson.*

Here's Charlie Tuna "unbagged." He said eight different phrases in his T.V. commercial voice. He was a very popular advertising doll; perhaps a customer would have sent in many product labels to get him. $100-150. *Courtesy Carmen Tickle Collection. Photo by Cris Johnson.*

This Libby's Advertising doll from 1970 was put out by Libby's canning company. She said eight different phrases like, "When it says Libby's, Libby's, Libby's on the label, label, label." A customer may have had to send in as many as twenty-five product labels to receive this doll free in a promotion. $50-75. *Courtesy Cris Johnson Collection. Photo by Cris Johnson.*

This is the back of the Santa Claus that was available from Gulf & Western. His construction was like the many Patter Pillows produced by Mattel. He was available during Christmas 1969 and 1970.

Santa Claus was the Christmas advertising doll for Gulf & Western. One needed only fill their car at a Gulf Gas station, and for a very small price could get Santa. Most of the advertising dolls are rare, as they were not for sale in department stores. Santa, however, was later available through the Montgomery Wards catalogue. $75-100.

The Pillsbury Dough Boy doll is modeled after the familiar advertising character "Poppin' Fresh" from the Pillsbury Company. He said eight different phrases in his commercial voice. Many product labels could be sent in to receive this doll. $100-150. *Photo by Sean Kettelkamp.*

In 1980 Mattel gave permission to Yesterday's Child to produce a porcelain version of Chatty Cathy. Their attempt to recapture the essence of Chatty Cathy fell short of collectors' aspirations, however. The doll said six phrases when her string was pulled, but her resemblance to the original Chatty Cathy was slight. Yesterday's Child did do a great job, however, with a porcelain version of the Ideal Toy Company's, "Crissy." $500 and up for the porcelain Chatty Cathy. *Courtesy Cris Johnson Collection. Photo by Cris Johnson.*

Chatty Patty #7023 was issued in 1983. This doll was the same as Peachy and her Puppets from 1973. The gimmick here was that Chatty Patty came with six different props that she could "hold" and talk about. She stood 16.5" tall and spoke ten different phrases in all. This doll seems to be the end of the "Chatty era," for Mattel has not had another doll named Chatty since. $50-75.